סליחות קורן ללילה הראשון • מנהג אנגליה

The Koren Seliḥot for the First Night • Minhag Anglia

קוֹרֶן יְרוּשָׁלַיִם

Office *of* The
CHIEF RABBI

The US
LIVING • LEARNING • CARING

סליחות קורן ללילה הראשון
THE KOREN SELIḤOT
FOR THE FIRST NIGHT

חטאנו
צורנו
סלח לנו
יוצרנו

WITH INTRODUCTION AND COMMENTARY BY

Chief Rabbi Ephraim Mirvis שליט״א

SELIḤOT TRANSLATION BY

Sara Daniel

•

KOREN PUBLISHERS JERUSALEM

The Koren Seliḥot for the First Night
First UK Hebrew/English Edition, 2016

Koren Publishers Jerusalem Ltd.
POB 4044, Jerusalem 91040, ISRAEL
POB 8531, New Milford, CT 06776, USA

www.korenpub.com

Koren Tanakh Font © 1962, 2016 Koren Publishers Jerusalem Ltd.
Koren Siddur Font and text design © 1981, 2016 Koren Publishers Jerusalem Ltd.
Introduction and commentary © 2016 Ephraim Mirvis
Seliḥot translation © 2016 Koren Publishers Jerusalem Ltd.

The English tefilla translation in this edition is based on the English translation
first published in Great Britain in 2006 in the Authorised Daily Prayer
Book of the United Hebrew Congregations of the Commonwealth: New Translation
and Commentary by Chief Rabbi Jonathan Sacks, (Fourth Edition, Compilation
© United Synagogue) by Collins, a division of HarperCollins Publishers, London.

Printed in the USA

Personal Size, Hardcover, ISBN 978 965 301 865 5

SEL1MA01

INTRODUCTION

A story is told of parents who were losing control of their unruly, young son. The father came up with an idea. He hung a plank of wood on a wall in their home, and every time his son misbehaved a nail was knocked into the wood. Over time, the child, filled with remorse, saw the impact of what he was doing and began to turn over a new leaf. Many days went by without any further nails being knocked into the wood. Proud of being a reformed character, the child then pleaded with his father to remove the nails. The delighted father obliged but then the boy promptly burst into tears. "What's the problem?" asked the father. The boy replied, "We can still see the holes in the wood where the nails used to be!" "I'm sorry," said the father, "there's nothing I can do about that."

Through the process of *teshuva*, our Father in Heaven guarantees that not only are the nails removed, but the holes disappear as well. We are given a fresh opportunity to engage constructively with life, and with complete and honest *teshuva*, the slate is wiped clean.

This is the idea that God conveyed to Moses after the sin of the golden calf, when He said "*Salaḥti kidvarekha* – I forgive you as you have requested," and it is the very essence of *Seliḥot*.

In this spirit, the Thirteen Attributes of Mercy are the core of our *Seliḥot* prayers. These words were taught by the Almighty to Moses for the people to use whenever they would seek divine compassion. Based on the Torah text in Exodus 34:5–7, Rabbi Yoḥanan (*Rosh HaShana* 17b) explains that it was as though the Almighty had wrapped Himself in a tallit just as a *ḥazan* leading the congregation would do, and demonstrated to Moses the proper order of prayers, and said, "Any time the people of Israel sins, let them recite this order of prayer and I will forgive them."

This reassurance that God forever awaits our return is the inspiration for our *Seliḥot* services, comprising penitential poems and prayers for the High Holy Days and other times of the year. The term "*Seliḥot*"

◀ refers

refers both to the poetic *piyutim* within the service as well as the title of the service itself.

The word "*seliḥa*" in the Torah has the connotation of absolute forgiveness. Calling our services "*Seliḥot*" is an optimistic statement through which we express our confidence that our heartfelt pleas for mercy, understanding and clemency will be positively received. This is consistent with the hopeful outlook we have always exhibited as a people, and it is an attitude that sustains and empowers us as we approach our annual days of reckoning.

How apt it is therefore that Psalm 27, which we recite at this time of year, concludes with the words "Hope in the LORD. Be strong and of good courage, and hope in the LORD." This same spirit of hopefulness and positivity characterises our *Seliḥot* services which, while being charged with full *kavana* – intention and fervour, reflect our expectations of a joyous outcome.

Similarly, a central prayer for "First Night *Seliḥot*" includes the refrain "*Lishmo'a el ha-rina ve'el ha-tefilla*" in which we call upon the Almighty to listen to the joyous praise that accompanies our prayers. Indeed, the hallmarks of a traditional *Seliḥot* service are passionate cries from the depths of our hearts, meaningful prayer, soulful melodies, and joyous outpourings of deep-rooted faith.

In recent years the opening *Seliḥot* service, traditionally held in Ashkenazi communities at midnight on a Saturday night prior to Rosh HaShana, has become a popular and key feature on our Synagogue calendar. Right around the Jewish world, many thousands of people usher in the High Holy Day season on this night in a spiritually uplifting and often life-enhancing manner, thanks to the evocative prayers and inspirational melodies included in the service. To date, there has been an absence of a specially prepared *Seliḥot* book exclusively for use on the first night. This volume, in seeking to address this need, carries with it a new translation and commentary to enhance the experience for congregants, and deepen awareness and understanding of the beautiful prayers.

I would like to extend particular thanks to Rabbi Daniel Roselaar for his scholarly input into this edition, together with Matthew Miller and everyone at Koren Publishers Jerusalem, particularly Esther Be'er and Rachel Meghnagi, who have diligently and expertly brought the idea to fruition.

◄ There are

There are two similar biblical terms – "*leha'azin*" meaning "to hear" and "*lishmo'a*," which means "to listen." *Leha'azin* indicates that the sounds have been registered but not necessarily internalised, and what has gone in one ear might just as easily have gone out of the other. *Lishmo'a*, however, implies focussed listening which leads to deep awareness and understanding. For this reason, the Almighty appeals to us: "*Shema Yisrael*" – "Listen, Israel: the LORD is our God, the LORD is One." In turn, on this night of *Seliḥot*, our central appeal to God is that He should be "*Shome'a*." We call out to Him: "*Lishmo'a el ha-rina*" – "please listen to our joyous praise and prayer"; "*Shema Kolenu*" – "Listen to our voice, LORD our God. Spare us and have compassion on us."

It is my fervent hope that the Almighty will, indeed, listen to our heartfelt *Seliḥot* prayers, and will bless us and all the people of Israel with a happy, successful, fulfilling and peaceful New Year.

Chief Rabbi Ephraim Mirvis
London, 5776 (2016)

FOREWORD

In Jewish communities across the world, the occasion of "Midnight *Seliḥot*" has become ever increasingly popular. Its late start time and proximity to the High Holy Day period set it apart from other, more conventional prayer services, and it is now firmly established as the curtain raiser for the spiritual journey that one undertakes from Rosh HaShana right through to Simḥat Torah. For those who embrace it, it is an evening of beautiful melodies, intense sanctity and an infectious sense of occasion.

As the impact of the service has grown, so too has the need for a publication to go along with it, and I am delighted that the United Synagogue has been able to play a part in delivering such a publication. Chief Rabbi Mirvis has spoken often about the need to make prayer more accessible and more relevant to our communities and, as ever, he has led from the front in making the first night of *Seliḥot* among the most uplifting and anticipated in the communal calendar.

It is my sincere hope and prayer that this edition of the *Koren Seliḥot for the First Night* will help further realise that vision for our communities and across the Jewish world for many years to come.

Stephen Pack
President, The United Synagogue
London, 5776 (2016)

סליחות ללילה הראשון

SELIHOT FOR THE FIRST NIGHT

Selihot for the First Night

אַשְׁרֵי Happy are those who dwell in Your House;   *Ps. 84*
they shall continue to praise You, Selah!
Happy are the people for whom this is so;   *Ps. 144*
happy are the people whose God is the LORD.
A song of praise by David.   *Ps. 145*

I will exalt You, my God, the King, and bless Your name for ever
and all time. Every day I will bless You, and praise Your name for
ever and all time. Great is the LORD and greatly to be praised;
His greatness is unfathomable. One generation will praise Your
works to the next, and tell of Your mighty deeds. On the glorious splendour of Your majesty I will meditate, and on the acts
of Your wonders. They shall talk of the power of Your awesome deeds, and I will tell of Your greatness. They shall recite
the record of Your great goodness, and sing with joy of Your
righteousness. The LORD is gracious and compassionate, slow
to anger and great in loving-kindness. The LORD is good to all,
and His compassion extends to all His works. All Your works
shall thank You, LORD, and Your devoted ones shall bless You.
They shall talk of the glory of Your kingship, and speak of Your
might. To make known to mankind His mighty deeds and the
glorious majesty of His kingship. Your kingdom is an everlasting kingdom, and Your reign is for all generations. The LORD
supports all who fall, and raises all who are bowed down. All
raise their eyes to You in hope, and You give them their food in
due season. You open Your hand, and satisfy every living thing

---

times daily guarantees eternal life for the soul. In the daily Shaharit service,
Ashrei serves as both an introduction and conclusion to the main part of the
service and it also introduces the daily Minha prayers. The Talmud stresses
the importance of this psalm in the context of its two special characteristics,
the alphabetical arrangement of the verses and the statement "פּוֹתֵחַ אֶת־יָדֶךָ,

סליחות ללילה הראשון

תהלים פד

תהלים קמד

תהלים קמה

אַשְׁרֵי יוֹשְׁבֵי בֵיתֶךָ, עוֹד יְהַלְלוּךָ סֶּלָה:

אַשְׁרֵי הָעָם שֶׁכָּכָה לּוֹ, אַשְׁרֵי הָעָם שֶׁיהוה אֱלֹהָיו:

תְּהִלָּה לְדָוִד

אֲרוֹמִמְךָ אֱלוֹהַי הַמֶּלֶךְ, וַאֲבָרְכָה שִׁמְךָ לְעוֹלָם וָעֶד:

בְּכָל־יוֹם אֲבָרְכֶךָּ, וַאֲהַלְלָה שִׁמְךָ לְעוֹלָם וָעֶד:

גָּדוֹל יהוה וּמְהֻלָּל מְאֹד, וְלִגְדֻלָּתוֹ אֵין חֵקֶר:

דּוֹר לְדוֹר יְשַׁבַּח מַעֲשֶׂיךָ, וּגְבוּרֹתֶיךָ יַגִּידוּ:

הֲדַר כְּבוֹד הוֹדֶךָ, וְדִבְרֵי נִפְלְאֹתֶיךָ אָשִׂיחָה:

וֶעֱזוּז נוֹרְאֹתֶיךָ יֹאמֵרוּ, וּגְדוּלָּתְךָ אֲסַפְּרֶנָּה:

זֵכֶר רַב־טוּבְךָ יַבִּיעוּ, וְצִדְקָתְךָ יְרַנֵּנוּ:

חַנּוּן וְרַחוּם יהוה, אֶרֶךְ אַפַּיִם וּגְדָל־חָסֶד:

טוֹב־יהוה לַכֹּל, וְרַחֲמָיו עַל־כָּל־מַעֲשָׂיו:

יוֹדוּךָ יהוה כָּל־מַעֲשֶׂיךָ, וַחֲסִידֶיךָ יְבָרְכוּכָה:

כְּבוֹד מַלְכוּתְךָ יֹאמֵרוּ, וּגְבוּרָתְךָ יְדַבֵּרוּ:

לְהוֹדִיעַ לִבְנֵי הָאָדָם גְּבוּרֹתָיו, וּכְבוֹד הֲדַר מַלְכוּתוֹ:

מַלְכוּתְךָ מַלְכוּת כָּל־עֹלָמִים, וּמֶמְשַׁלְתְּךָ בְּכָל־דּוֹר וָדֹר:

סוֹמֵךְ יהוה לְכָל־הַנֹּפְלִים, וְזוֹקֵף לְכָל־הַכְּפוּפִים:

עֵינֵי־כֹל אֵלֶיךָ יְשַׂבֵּרוּ, וְאַתָּה נוֹתֵן־לָהֶם אֶת־אָכְלָם בְּעִתּוֹ:

פּוֹתֵחַ אֶת־יָדֶךָ, וּמַשְׂבִּיעַ לְכָל־חַי רָצוֹן:

אַשְׁרֵי *Happy are those.* Our High Holy Day *Seliḥot* services commence with Psalm 145, probably the most recited of the 150 psalms. Highlighting its importance, the Talmud (*Berakhot* 4b) states that reciting this passage three

with favour. The LORD is righteous in all His ways, and kind
in all He does. The LORD is close to all who call on Him, to all
who call on Him in truth. He fulfils the will of those who revere
Him; He hears their cry and saves them. The LORD guards all
who love Him, but all the wicked He will destroy. ▸ My mouth
shall speak the praise of the LORD, and all creatures shall bless
His holy name for ever and all time.

We will bless the LORD now and for ever. Halleluya!   *Ps. 115*

Some say in an undertone:

וְעַתָּה And now, let the power of my Master be great,   *Num. 14*
as You promised, declaring:

Remember, LORD, Your compassion and loving-kindness,   *Ps. 25*
for they are everlasting.

HALF KADDISH

Leader: יִתְגַּדַּל Magnified and sanctified may His great name be,
in the world He created by His will.
May He establish His kingdom
in your lifetime and in your days,
and in the lifetime of all the house of Israel,
swiftly and soon – and say: Amen.

All: May His great name be blessed for ever and all time.

Leader: Blessed and praised, glorified and exalted,
raised and honoured, uplifted and lauded
be the name of the Holy One, blessed be He,
beyond any blessing,
song, praise and consolation
uttered in the world – and say: Amen.

KADDISH.

The Kaddish prayer is often thought of as a mourner's prayer – its lofty praises
of God are well-suited to mourners who express their fealty to the Almighty,
even under difficult personal circumstances. However, its role as such did

צַדִּיק יהוה בְּכָל־דְּרָכָיו, וְחָסִיד בְּכָל־מַעֲשָׂיו:

קָרוֹב יהוה לְכָל־קֹרְאָיו, לְכֹל אֲשֶׁר יִקְרָאֻהוּ בֶאֱמֶת:

רְצוֹן־יְרֵאָיו יַעֲשֶׂה, וְאֶת־שַׁוְעָתָם יִשְׁמַע, וְיוֹשִׁיעֵם:

שׁוֹמֵר יהוה אֶת־כָּל־אֹהֲבָיו, וְאֵת כָּל־הָרְשָׁעִים יַשְׁמִיד:

‹ תְּהִלַּת יהוה יְדַבֶּר פִּי, וִיבָרֵךְ כָּל־בָּשָׂר שֵׁם קָדְשׁוֹ לְעוֹלָם וָעֶד:

תהלים קטו

וַאֲנַחְנוּ נְבָרֵךְ יָהּ מֵעַתָּה וְעַד־עוֹלָם, הַלְלוּיָהּ:

Some say in an undertone:

במדבר יד

וְעַתָּה יִגְדַּל־נָא כֹּחַ אֲדֹנָי כַּאֲשֶׁר דִּבַּרְתָּ לֵאמֹר:

תהלים כה

זְכֹר־רַחֲמֶיךָ יהוה וַחֲסָדֶיךָ כִּי מֵעוֹלָם הֵמָּה:

חצי קדיש

ש״ץ: יִתְגַּדַּל וְיִתְקַדַּשׁ שְׁמֵהּ רַבָּא (קהל: אָמֵן)

בְּעָלְמָא דִּי בְרָא כִרְעוּתֵהּ

וְיַמְלִיךְ מַלְכוּתֵהּ

בְּחַיֵּיכוֹן וּבְיוֹמֵיכוֹן וּבְחַיֵּי דְכָל בֵּית יִשְׂרָאֵל

בַּעֲגָלָא וּבִזְמַן קָרִיב, וְאִמְרוּ אָמֵן. (קהל: אָמֵן)

קהל
 וש״ץ: יְהֵא שְׁמֵהּ רַבָּא מְבָרַךְ לְעָלַם וּלְעָלְמֵי עָלְמַיָּא.

ש״ץ: יִתְבָּרַךְ וְיִשְׁתַּבַּח וְיִתְפָּאַר וְיִתְרוֹמַם וְיִתְנַשֵּׂא

וְיִתְהַדָּר וְיִתְעַלֶּה וְיִתְהַלָּל

שְׁמֵהּ דְּקֻדְשָׁא בְּרִיךְ הוּא (קהל: בְּרִיךְ הוּא)

לְעֵלָּא מִן כָּל בִּרְכָתָא וְשִׁירָתָא, תֻּשְׁבְּחָתָא וְנֶחֱמָתָא

דִּי אֲמִירָן בְּעָלְמָא, וְאִמְרוּ אָמֵן. (קהל: אָמֵן)

You open Your hand," which conveys the notion that Divine Providence cares
for everything that lives.

לְךָ You are right, my Master, and we are shamefaced. *Dan. 9*
How can we complain? What can we say?
What can we plead? How can we justify ourselves?
Let us search our ways and examine them and return to You,
 for Your right hand is outstretched to receive those who return.
Without goodness or worthy deeds we have come before You,
 Like paupers, like the destitute, we knock at your door.
At your door we knock, O compassionate, gracious One,
Please, do not turn us away from You empty-handed.
▸ From before You, our King, do not turn us away empty-handed,
 for You listen to prayer.

שֹׁמֵעַ תְּפִלָּה You who listen to prayer – all creatures of flesh will come to *Ps. 65*
 You.
All creatures of flesh will come and bow down before You, O LORD.
They will come and bow down before You, my Master, and give honour *Ps. 86*
 to Your name.
Come, let us bow in worship, bend our knees before the LORD our *Ps. 95*
 Maker.

---

the beginning of Elul to Yom Kippur. Some of this passage may have been
excerpted from a longer *piyut* (liturgical poem) that is no longer recited. The
opening line declares that God is unquestioningly righteous, whilst we are
ashamed of our sins. The latter lines present an image of the Jewish people
approaching the Almighty like paupers who knock on the door of a wealthy
benefactor, hoping not to be turned away empty-handed. Instead of asking
for money or provisions we come to seek forgiveness.

שֹׁמֵעַ תְּפִלָּה *You who listen to prayer.* The formal *Seliḥot* are preceded here by a
selection of more than forty biblical verses which praise God as the mighty
Ruler of the universe. Rav Joseph B. Soloveitchik explained that the structure
of the *Seliḥot* service is modelled on the structure of our daily prayer services and, just as the requests contained in the middle *berakhot* (blessings)
of the Amida prayer are always preceded by blessings which praise God,
so too, the requests for forgiveness that form the bulk of the *Seliḥot*, must
be preceded by verses of praise. We use the beautiful biblical expressions
of praise, written by psalmists and prophets who were imbued with the
divine spirit.

לְךָ אֲדֹנָי הַצְּדָקָה, וְלָנוּ בְּשֶׁת הַפָּנִים:
מַה נִּתְאוֹנֵן וּמַה נֹּאמַר, מַה נְּדַבֵּר וּמַה נִּצְטַדָּק:
נַחְפְּשָׂה דְרָכֵינוּ וְנַחְקוֹרָה וְנָשׁוּבָה אֵלֶיךָ:
כִּי יְמִינְךָ פְּשׁוּטָה לְקַבֵּל שָׁבִים.
לֹא בְחֶסֶד וְלֹא בְמַעֲשִׂים בָּאנוּ לְפָנֶיךָ
כְּדַלִּים וּכְרָשִׁים דָּפַקְנוּ דְלָתֶיךָ.
דְּלָתֶיךָ דָּפַקְנוּ רַחוּם וְחַנּוּן
נָא אַל תְּשִׁיבֵנוּ רֵיקָם מִלְּפָנֶיךָ.
‹ מִלְּפָנֶיךָ מַלְכֵּנוּ רֵיקָם אַל תְּשִׁיבֵנוּ
כִּי אַתָּה שׁוֹמֵעַ תְּפִלָּה.

שֹׁמֵעַ תְּפִלָּה, עָדֶיךָ כָּל־בָּשָׂר יָבֹאוּ:

יָבוֹא כָל בָּשָׂר לְהִשְׁתַּחֲוֹת לְפָנֶיךָ יהוה.
יָבוֹאוּ וְיִשְׁתַּחֲווּ לְפָנֶיךָ אֲדֹנָי, וִיכַבְּדוּ לִשְׁמֶךָ:

בֹּאוּ נִשְׁתַּחֲוֶה וְנִכְרָעָה, נִבְרְכָה לִפְנֵי־יהוה עֹשֵׂנוּ:

---

not develop until the Middle Ages. As some mourners were unable to lead a full service, all mourners were invited to lead the congregation in the recitation of this important prayer, in their quest to add merit to the memory of the deceased. First and foremost, Kaddish is a proclamation of the sanctity and greatness of the Almighty and it expresses our aspiration for His name to be exalted throughout the universe. The opening words are based on a verse in the book of Ezekiel (38:23) and the prayer is principally written in Aramaic, indicating that it was composed in Babylonia during the Amoraic era (c200–500 CE). Kaddish generally serves as a punctuation mark in our services, with a "Half Kaddish" introducing the key section of every *tefilla*, as is the case here, and a "Full Kaddish" indicating the conclusion of the main components of the service.

לְךָ אֲדֹנָי הַצְּדָקָה *You are right, my Master.* These introductory verses appear at the commencement of the *Seliḥot* throughout the penitential period, from

Come, let us enter His dwelling, bow before His footstool. *Ps. 132*

Come in at His gates with thanksgiving; come to His courts with praise. *Ps. 100*
Thank Him and bless His name.

As for us, in Your great loving-kindness we will come into Your House;
we will bow down to Your holy Temple in awe of You.

Come, bless the LORD, all you servants of the LORD, who nightly stand *Ps. 134*
in the House of the LORD.

Lift up your hands towards the Sanctuary and bless the LORD.

Exalt the LORD our God, and bow before His footstool – He is holy. *Ps. 99*

Exalt the LORD our God, and bow at His holy mountain, for holy is the *Ibid.*
LORD our God.

Bow down to the LORD in the splendour of holiness; tremble before *Ps. 96*
Him, all the earth.

We will bow down to Your holy Temple and give thanks to Your name
for Your loving-kindness and truth, for You have magnified Your
name and Your word above all else.

LORD, God of hosts, who is like You – Mighty One, LORD, with Your *Ps. 89*
faithfulness all around You?

For who in the heavens may be compared to the LORD; who is like the *Ibid.*
LORD among the angels?

For You are great, and You do wonders, You are God alone. *Ps. 86*

For Your loving-kindness reaches over heaven itself, and Your truth as *Ps. 108*
high as the skies.

Great is the LORD and greatly to be praised; His greatness cannot be *Ps. 145*
fathomed.

For great is the LORD and greatly to be praised; He is awesome beyond *1 Chr. 16*
all heavenly powers.

For the LORD is the great God, the King great above all heavenly powers. *Ps. 95*

Who is the god, in heaven or on earth, who can perform works and *Deut. 3*
mighty acts like Yours?

Who would not hold You in awe, King of the nations, for that befits You, *Jer. 10*
for among all the wise people of nations, in all their realms, there is
none like You.

There is none like You, LORD; You are great, and Your name is great in
its might.

תהלים קלב
נָבוֹאָה לְמִשְׁכְּנוֹתָיו, נִשְׁתַּחֲוֶה לַהֲדֹם רַגְלָיו:

תהלים ק
בֹּאוּ שְׁעָרָיו בְּתוֹדָה חֲצֵרֹתָיו בִּתְהִלָּה, הוֹדוּ לוֹ בָּרְכוּ שְׁמוֹ:

וַאֲנַחְנוּ בְּרֹב חַסְדְּךָ נָבוֹא בֵיתֶךָ

נִשְׁתַּחֲוֶה אֶל הֵיכַל קָדְשְׁךָ בְּיִרְאָתֶךָ.

תהלים קלד
הִנֵּה בָּרְכוּ אֶת־יהוה כָּל־עַבְדֵי יהוה

הָעֹמְדִים בְּבֵית־יהוה בַּלֵּילוֹת:

שְׂאוּ־יְדֵכֶם קֹדֶשׁ, וּבָרְכוּ אֶת־יהוה:

תהלים צט
רוֹמְמוּ יהוה אֱלֹהֵינוּ וְהִשְׁתַּחֲווּ לַהֲדֹם רַגְלָיו, קָדוֹשׁ הוּא:

רוֹמְמוּ יהוה אֱלֹהֵינוּ וְהִשְׁתַּחֲווּ לְהַר קָדְשׁוֹ

כִּי־קָדוֹשׁ יהוה אֱלֹהֵינוּ:

תהלים צו
הִשְׁתַּחֲווּ לַיהוה בְּהַדְרַת־קֹדֶשׁ, חִילוּ מִפָּנָיו כָּל־הָאָרֶץ:

נִשְׁתַּחֲוֶה אֶל הֵיכַל קָדְשְׁךָ וְנוֹדֶה אֶת שְׁמֶךָ

עַל חַסְדְּךָ וְעַל אֲמִתֶּךָ, כִּי הִגְדַּלְתָּ עַל כָּל שִׁמְךָ אִמְרָתֶךָ.

תהלים פט
יהוה אֱלֹהֵי צְבָאוֹת מִי־כָמוֹךָ חֲסִין יָהּ, וֶאֱמוּנָתְךָ סְבִיבוֹתֶיךָ:

כִּי מִי בַשַּׁחַק יַעֲרֹךְ לַיהוה, יִדְמֶה לַיהוה בִּבְנֵי אֵלִים:

תהלים פו
כִּי־גָדוֹל אַתָּה וְעֹשֵׂה נִפְלָאוֹת, אַתָּה אֱלֹהִים לְבַדֶּךָ:

תהלים קח
כִּי־גָדוֹל מֵעַל־שָׁמַיִם חַסְדֶּךָ, וְעַד־שְׁחָקִים אֲמִתֶּךָ:

תהלים קמה
גָּדוֹל יהוה וּמְהֻלָּל מְאֹד, וְלִגְדֻלָּתוֹ אֵין חֵקֶר:

תהלים צו
כִּי גָדוֹל יהוה וּמְהֻלָּל מְאֹד, נוֹרָא הוּא עַל־כָּל־אֱלֹהִים:

תהלים צה
כִּי אֵל גָּדוֹל יהוה, וּמֶלֶךְ גָּדוֹל עַל־כָּל־אֱלֹהִים:

דברים ג
אֲשֶׁר מִי־אֵל בַּשָּׁמַיִם וּבָאָרֶץ אֲשֶׁר־יַעֲשֶׂה כְמַעֲשֶׂיךָ וְכִגְבוּרֹתֶךָ:

ירמיה י
מִי לֹא יִרָאֲךָ מֶלֶךְ הַגּוֹיִם כִּי לְךָ יָאָתָה

כִּי בְכָל־חַכְמֵי הַגּוֹיִם וּבְכָל־מַלְכוּתָם מֵאֵין כָּמוֹךָ:

מֵאֵין כָּמוֹךָ יהוה, גָּדוֹל אַתָּה וְגָדוֹל שִׁמְךָ בִּגְבוּרָה:

Your arm is mighty; Your hand holds its power, Your right hand raised. *Ps. 89*

The day is Yours, and Yours is the night; You established light and the sun. *Ps. 74*

In His hands are the depths of the earth, and the mountain peaks are His. *Ps. 95*

Who can tell of the Lᴏʀᴅ's mighty acts and make all His praises heard? *Ps. 106*

Yours, Lᴏʀᴅ, are the greatness and the power, the glory and the majesty *1 Chr. 29*
and splendour, for everything in heaven and earth is Yours.

Yours, Lᴏʀᴅ, is the kingdom; You are exalted as Head over all.

The heavens are Yours, and Yours is the earth; the world and all that is *Ps. 89*
in it – it is You who founded them.

You laid out the boundaries of the earth; summer and winter – it is You *Ps. 74*
who formed them.

You shattered the sea with Your might; You broke the sea-monsters'
heads on the water.

You shattered the Leviathan's heads; You turned him into food for
desert creatures.

You split the channels of spring and stream, You dried up mighty rivers.

You rule over the surge of the sea; as its waves swell, it is You who still *Ps. 89*
them.

Great is the Lᴏʀᴅ and greatly to be praised in the city of God, on His *Ps. 48*
holy mountain.

Lᴏʀᴅ of hosts, the God of Israel, enthroned above the Cherubim, You *Is. 37*
are God alone.

God who is revered in a company of many holy ones, awesome over all *Ps. 89*
that surrounds Him.

The heavens will declare Your wonders, Lᴏʀᴅ, and Your faithfulness, in
the assembly of holy ones.

Come, let us sing for joy to the Lᴏʀᴅ; let us shout aloud to the Rock of *Ps. 95*
our salvation.

Let us greet Him with thanksgiving, shout aloud to Him in songs of
praise.

Righteousness and justice are the foundation of Your throne; kindness *Ps. 89*
and truth come out to greet You.

Together we made sweet company; in a great crowd we came to the *Ps. 55*
House of God.

The sea is His, He made it; the dry land too, for His hands formed it. *Ps. 95*

In His hand is every living soul, the breath of all mankind. *Job 12*

לְךָ זְרוֹעַ עִם־גְּבוּרָה, תָּעֹז יָדְךָ תָּרוּם יְמִינֶךָ:

לְךָ יוֹם אַף־לְךָ לָיְלָה, אַתָּה הֲכִינוֹתָ מָאוֹר וָשָׁמֶשׁ:

אֲשֶׁר בְּיָדוֹ מֶחְקְרֵי־אָרֶץ, וְתוֹעֲפוֹת הָרִים לוֹ:

מִי יְמַלֵּל גְּבוּרוֹת יהוה, יַשְׁמִיעַ כָּל־תְּהִלָּתוֹ:

לְךָ יהוה הַגְּדֻלָּה וְהַגְּבוּרָה וְהַתִּפְאֶרֶת וְהַנֵּצַח וְהַהוֹד

כִּי־כֹל בַּשָּׁמַיִם וּבָאָרֶץ, לְךָ יהוה הַמַּמְלָכָה וְהַמִּתְנַשֵּׂא
לְכֹל לְרֹאשׁ:

לְךָ שָׁמַיִם אַף־לְךָ אָרֶץ, תֵּבֵל וּמְלֹאָהּ אַתָּה יְסַדְתָּם:

אַתָּה הִצַּבְתָּ כָּל־גְּבוּלוֹת אָרֶץ, קַיִץ וָחֹרֶף אַתָּה יְצַרְתָּם:

אַתָּה פוֹרַרְתָּ בְעָזְּךָ יָם, שִׁבַּרְתָּ רָאשֵׁי תַנִּינִים עַל־הַמָּיִם:

אַתָּה רִצַּצְתָּ רָאשֵׁי לִוְיָתָן, תִּתְּנֶנּוּ מַאֲכָל לְעָם לְצִיִּים:

אַתָּה בָקַעְתָּ מַעְיָן וָנָחַל, אַתָּה הוֹבַשְׁתָּ נַהֲרוֹת אֵיתָן:

אַתָּה מוֹשֵׁל בְּגֵאוּת הַיָּם, בְּשׂוֹא גַלָּיו אַתָּה תְשַׁבְּחֵם:

גָּדוֹל יהוה וּמְהֻלָּל מְאֹד, בְּעִיר אֱלֹהֵינוּ הַר־קָדְשׁוֹ:

יהוה צְבָאוֹת אֱלֹהֵי יִשְׂרָאֵל יֹשֵׁב הַכְּרֻבִים
אַתָּה־הוּא הָאֱלֹהִים לְבַדְּךָ:

אֵל נַעֲרָץ בְּסוֹד־קְדֹשִׁים רַבָּה, וְנוֹרָא עַל־כָּל־סְבִיבָיו:

וְיוֹדוּ שָׁמַיִם פִּלְאֲךָ יהוה, אַף־אֱמוּנָתְךָ בִּקְהַל קְדֹשִׁים:

לְכוּ נְרַנְּנָה לַיהוה, נָרִיעָה לְצוּר יִשְׁעֵנוּ:

נְקַדְּמָה פָנָיו בְּתוֹדָה, בִּזְמִרוֹת נָרִיעַ לוֹ:

צֶדֶק וּמִשְׁפָּט מְכוֹן כִּסְאֶךָ, חֶסֶד וֶאֱמֶת יְקַדְּמוּ פָנֶיךָ:

אֲשֶׁר יַחְדָּו נַמְתִּיק סוֹד, בְּבֵית אֱלֹהִים נְהַלֵּךְ בְּרָגֶשׁ:

אֲשֶׁר־לוֹ הַיָּם וְהוּא עָשָׂהוּ, וְיַבֶּשֶׁת יָדָיו יָצָרוּ:

אֲשֶׁר בְּיָדוֹ נֶפֶשׁ כָּל־חָי, וְרוּחַ כָּל־בְּשַׂר־אִישׁ:

‣ הַנְּשָׁמָה לָךְ The spirit is Yours, and the body Your creation;
spare those You have formed.
The spirit is Yours, and the body is Yours;
Lord, act for the sake of Your name.
We have come because of Your name, Lord;
act for the sake of Your name.
For the glory of Your name, for Your name is Gracious
and Compassionate God.
For the sake of Your name, Lord,
forgive our iniquity, though it is great.

The congregation then the Leader:

סְלַח לָנוּ Forgive us, our Father,
for in our great foolishness we have blundered.
Pardon us, our King,
for our iniquities are many.

אֵיךְ נִפְתַּח How can we open our mouths before You,
O Dweller of the spread out Heavens?
How can we face You, and pour out prayer?
We have defiled Your straight, decent ways,
We have clung to abominations,
and deeds that must be renounced.
We have trailed after false delusions and deceptions,
We have been stubborn and insolent,
Because of us, You raged against Your secure haven,
Now it is destroyed; its sweet savour has ceased.
Dispersed and unsettled are the anointed priests,
Who know how to perform offerings and sacrifices,
How we were chastised by envoys and messengers –
Yet we would not heed or hear reproach.
And ever since, we have been driven far away,
Murdered, massacred, slaughtered,
Only a few have survived amongst the thorns,
Our eyes have dimmed without finding relief.

‹ הַנְּשָׁמָה לָךְ וְהַגּוּף פָּעֳלָךְ, חוּסָה עַל עֲמָלָךְ.
הַנְּשָׁמָה לָךְ וְהַגּוּף שֶׁלָּךְ, יהוה עֲשֵׂה לְמַעַן שְׁמֶךָ.
אָתָאנוּ עַל שִׁמְךָ, יהוה עֲשֵׂה לְמַעַן שְׁמֶךָ
בַּעֲבוּר כְּבוֹד שִׁמְךָ, כִּי אֵל חַנּוּן וְרַחוּם שְׁמֶךָ.
לְמַעַן שִׁמְךָ יהוה, וְסָלַחְתָּ לַעֲוֺנֵנוּ כִּי רַב הוּא.

שְׁלִיחַ צִבּוּר then the קָהָל The:

סְלַח לָנוּ, אָבִינוּ, כִּי בְרֹב אִוַּלְתֵּנוּ שָׁגִינוּ.
מְחַל לָנוּ, מַלְכֵּנוּ, כִּי רַבּוּ עֲוֺנֵינוּ.

אֵיךְ נִפְתַּח פֶּה לְפָנֶיךָ, דַּר מְתוּחִים
בְּאֵילוּ פָנִים נִשְׁפָּךְ שִׂיחִים.
גָּעֳלֽוּ נְתִיבוֹתֶיךָ הַיְשָׁרִים וְהַנְּכוֹחִים
דָּבַקְנוּ בְּתוֹעֵבוֹת וּבְמַעֲשִׂים זְנוּחִים.
הָלַכְנוּ אַחֲרֵי מַשְׂאוֹת שָׁוְא וּמַדּוּחִים
וְהִקְשִׁינוּ עֹרֶף וְהֶעֱזֽנוּ מְצָחִים.
זָעַמְתָּ בְּשֶׁלָּנוּ בֵּית מִשְׁכְּנוֹת מִבְטָחִים
חָרַב, וּפַס רֵיחַ נִיחוֹחִים.
טֹרְדוּ וְטֻלְטְלוּ כֹּהֲנִים הַמְשׁוּחִים
יוֹדְעֵי עֵרֶךְ עוֹלוֹת וּזְבָחִים.
כַּמָּה יִסַּרְתָּנוּ עַל יְדֵי צִירִים וּשְׁלוּחִים
לֹא הִקְשַׁבְנוּ לַמּוֹרִים וְלִשְׁמֹעַ לַמּוֹכִיחִים.
מֵאָז וְעַד עַתָּה אָנוּ נִדָּחִים
נֶהֱרָגִים נִשְׁחָטִים וְנִטְבָּחִים.
שָׂרַדְנוּ מְתֵי מְעַט בֵּין קוֹצִים כְּסוּחִים
עֵינֵינוּ כָלוֹת לִמְצֹא רְוָחִים.

The oppressors of Your people,
Who pray to foreign gods,
Morning and evening – why do they succeed?
They arise against You, uttering curses,
O battered and shattered ones,
in whom do you place your trust?
O Eternal, Holy Dweller, look upon the humiliation
of those who sigh,
Who rely upon You, and cling to You,
‣ With Your wondrous right hand,
we will be saved for all eternity,
For in Your abundant mercy we trust.

כִּי For it is in Your great compassion that we trust, / and on Your
righteousness that we lean;
and for Your forgiveness that we hope, / and for Your salvation that
we wait.
You are the King, who has always loved righteousness;
who forgives the iniquities of His people,
and removes the sins of those who hold Him in awe;
who has forged a covenant with ancestors,
and still keeps His promise to their last descendants.
It is You who descended in a cloud of Your glory to Mount Sinai,
and You showed the ways of Your goodness to Moses Your servant;
You revealed the ways of Your loving-kindness to him
and told him that You are a compassionate and gracious God,
slow to anger, abounding in loving-kindness
and abundantly doing good,
and directing all the world through Your attribute of compassion.
‣ And so it is written:

"And He said, I shall cause all My good to pass before you   *Ex. 33*
and I shall call out the Tetragrammaton before you,
and I will show grace to those I favour
and compassion to those I deem deserving of compassion."

פּוֹרְכֵי עַמְּךָ אֲשֶׁר לְבֵל שׁוֹחֲחִים
צָפַר וָעֶרֶב הוֹלְכִים וּמַצְלִיחִים.
קָמִים לְמוּלְךָ וְנִאָצוֹת שׁוֹחֲחִים
רְעוּצִים וּרְצוּצִים, בַּמֶּה אַתֶּם בּוֹטְחִים.
שׁוֹכֵן עַד וְקָדוֹשׁ, צָפָה בְּעֶלְבּוֹן אֲנוּחִים
תְּמוּכִים עָלֶיךָ וּלְךָ מִתְאַחִים.
‹ בְּנוֹרָאוֹת יְמִינְךָ נוּשַׁע לִנְצָחִים
כִּי עַל רַחֲמֶיךָ הָרַבִּים אָנוּ בְטוּחִים.

כִּי עַל רַחֲמֶיךָ הָרַבִּים אָנוּ בְטוּחִים, וְעַל צִדְקוֹתֶיךָ אָנוּ נִשְׁעָנִים
וְלִסְלִיחוֹתֶיךָ אָנוּ מְקַוִּים, וְלִישׁוּעָתְךָ אָנוּ מְצַפִּים.
אַתָּה הוּא מֶלֶךְ אוֹהֵב צְדָקוֹת מִקֶּדֶם
מַעֲבִיר עֲוֹנוֹת עַמּוֹ וּמֵסִיר חַטֹּאת יְרֵאָיו
כּוֹרֵת בְּרִית לָרִאשׁוֹנִים וּמְקַיֵּם שְׁבוּעָה לָאַחֲרוֹנִים.
אַתָּה הוּא שֶׁיָּרַדְתָּ בַּעֲנַן כְּבוֹדְךָ עַל הַר סִינַי
וְהֶרְאֵיתָ דַּרְכֵי טוּבְךָ לְמֹשֶׁה עַבְדֶּךָ.
אָרְחוֹת חֲסָדֶיךָ גִּלִּיתָ לּוֹ
וְהוֹדַעְתּוֹ כִּי אַתָּה אֵל רַחוּם וְחַנּוּן
אֶרֶךְ אַפַּיִם וְרַב חֶסֶד וּמַרְבֶּה לְהֵיטִיב
וּמַנְהִיג אֶת הָעוֹלָם כֻּלּוֹ בְּמִדַּת הָרַחֲמִים.
‹ וְכֵן כָּתוּב:

שמות לג

וַיֹּאמֶר אֲנִי אַעֲבִיר כָּל־טוּבִי עַל פָּנֶיךָ
וְקָרָאתִי בְשֵׁם יהוה לְפָנֶיךָ
וְחַנֹּתִי אֶת־אֲשֶׁר אָחֹן, וְרִחַמְתִּי אֶת־אֲשֶׁר אֲרַחֵם:

אֵל אֶֽרֶךְ God, You are a God slow to anger, You are called the Master of Compassion, and You have taught the way of repentance. May You remember today and every day the greatness of Your compassion and kindness, for the sake of the descendants of Your beloved ones. Turn toward us in compassion, for You are the Master of Compassion. We come before You in plea and prayer, as You in ancient times showed the humble one [Moses]. Turn from Your fierce anger, as is written in Your Torah. In the shadow of Your wings may we shelter and abide, as on the day when the LORD descended in the cloud. ‣ Overlook sin and wipe away guilt, as on the day when "He stood beside him there." Give ear to our pleading and listen to our speech, as on the day when "he called upon the name of the LORD," and in that place is said –

The congregation then the Leader:

וַיַּעֲבֹר And the LORD passed by before him and proclaimed: *Ex. 34*

All say aloud:

יהוה The LORD, the LORD, compassionate and gracious God,
slow to anger, abounding in loving-kindness and truth,
extending loving-kindness to a thousand generations, forgiving
iniquity, rebellion and sin, and absolving [the guilty who repent].

All continue:

Forgive us our iniquity and our sin,
and take us as Your inheritance.

סְלַח לָֽנוּ Forgive us, our Father, for we have sinned.
Pardon us, our King, for we have transgressed.
For You, Master, are good and forgiving,   *Ps. 86*
abounding in loving-kindness to all who call on You.

_____

The tetragrammaton (four-letter divine name), which describes God as a merciful deity, appears twice at the beginning of this declaration. The Talmud explains that the first "Hashem" refers to God before a person sins and the second "Hashem" refers to Him after one's repentance. This immensely powerful statement confirms that genuine penitents can restore their relationship with God to exactly what it was prior to their sin. When human relationships are damaged and repaired it is often difficult to restore the trust and love to exactly what had existed previously. But God is much more forgiving. If a

אֵל אֶרֶךְ אַפַּיִם אַתָּה, וּבַעַל הָרַחֲמִים נִקְרֵאתָ, וְדֶרֶךְ תְּשׁוּבָה
הוֹרֵיתָ. גְּדֻלַּת רַחֲמֶיךָ וַחֲסָדֶיךָ, תִּזְכֹּר הַיּוֹם וּבְכָל יוֹם לְזֶרַע
יְדִידֶיךָ. תֵּפֶן אֵלֵינוּ בְּרַחֲמִים, כִּי אַתָּה הוּא בַּעַל הָרַחֲמִים.
בְּתַחֲנוּן וּבִתְפִלָּה פָּנֶיךָ נְקַדֵּם, כְּהוֹדַעְתָּ לֶעָנָו מִקֶּדֶם. מֵחֲרוֹן
אַפְּךָ שׁוּב, כְּמוֹ בְּתוֹרָתְךָ כָּתוּב. וּבְצֵל כְּנָפֶיךָ נֶחֱסֶה וְנִתְלוֹנָן,
כְּיוֹם וַיֵּרֶד יהוה בֶּעָנָן. ‹ תַּעֲבֹר עַל פֶּשַׁע וְתִמְחֶה אָשָׁם, כְּיוֹם
וַיִּתְיַצֵּב עִמּוֹ שָׁם. תַּאֲזִין שַׁוְעָתֵנוּ וְתַקְשִׁיב מֶנּוּ מַאֲמָר, כְּיוֹם
וַיִּקְרָא בְשֵׁם יהוה, וְשָׁם נֶאֱמַר

שליח ציבור *then the* קהל *The*:

שמות לד

וַיַּעֲבֹר יהוה עַל־פָּנָיו וַיִּקְרָא

All say aloud:

יהוה, יהוה, אֵל רַחוּם וְחַנּוּן, אֶרֶךְ אַפַּיִם, וְרַב־חֶסֶד וֶאֱמֶת:
נֹצֵר חֶסֶד לָאֲלָפִים, נֹשֵׂא עָוֹן וָפֶשַׁע וְחַטָּאָה, וְנַקֵּה:

All continue:

וְסָלַחְתָּ לַעֲוֹנֵנוּ וּלְחַטָּאתֵנוּ, וּנְחַלְתָּנוּ:

סְלַח לָנוּ אָבִינוּ כִּי חָטָאנוּ, מְחַל לָנוּ מַלְכֵּנוּ כִּי פָשָׁעְנוּ.
כִּי־אַתָּה אֲדֹנָי טוֹב וְסַלָּח, וְרַב־חֶסֶד לְכָל־קֹרְאֶיךָ:

תהלים פו

יהוה, יהוה *The* Lord, *the* Lord. This passage comprises the Thirteen Attributes of Divine Mercy (*Yud-Gimmel Middot HaRaḥamim*) and is a repeated focus of the entire *Seliḥot* service. They appear in the Torah (Exodus 34:6–7) when Moses seeks forgiveness, on behalf of the children of Israel, for the sin of the golden calf. The Talmud (*Rosh HaShana* 17b) depicts God as assuming the role of a *ḥazan* leading the congregation in prayer. He promises the Jewish people that, should they recite these Attributes of Mercy in repentance, their sins will be forgiven. The verses are not a magical formula that guarantees automatic pardon. To be effective, they must be accompanied by genuine *teshuva*.

יהוה, בְּקֶר O Lord, at daybreak hear our voice;
at daybreak we plead before You and await (You).
Hear the sound of our supplication when we cry out to You;
when we raise up our hands towards Your sacred inner sanctuary.
Hear our voices, O Lord, when we cry out;
be gracious to us and answer us.
Restore us, O God of our salvation; revoke Your anger towards us.   *Ps. 85*
No one invokes Your name, rousing himself to take hold of You –   *Is. 64*
‣ Hear our prayer, O Lord; give ear to our plea;
do not be silent to our tears.

כְּרַחֵם As a father has compassion for his children,
so, Lord, have compassion for us.
Salvation belongs to the Lord;   *Ps. 3*
may Your blessing rest upon Your people, Selah!
The Lord of hosts is with us,   *Ps. 46*
the God of Jacob is our stronghold, Selah!
Lord of hosts: happy is the one who trusts in You.   *Ps. 84*
Lord, save! May the King answer us on the day we call.   *Ps. 20*

‣ סְלַח־נָא Forgive, please, this people's iniquity,   *Num. 14*
in the abundance of Your kindness,
and as You have forgiven this people
from the time of Egypt until now,
and there it is said:

Congregation then the Leader:
And the Lord said, I have forgiven as you asked.

הַטֵּה Give ear, my God and hear;   *Dan. 9*
open Your eyes and see our desolation, and the city that bears Your name,
for it is not on the strength of our righteousness
that we throw down our pleadings before You,
but on the strength of Your great compassion.

---

follows. It would be truly audacious for mere mortals to compose prayers
with the presumption that we know how best to approach God so that He
will respond favourably to our pleas. Thus, we commence with biblical verses
which masterfully articulate our thoughts and prayers at this time.

יהוה, בֹּקֶר תִּשְׁמַע קוֹלֵנוּ, בֹּקֶר נַעֲרָךְ־לְךָ וַנְצַפֶּה.
שְׁמַע קוֹל תַּחֲנוּנֵינוּ בְּשַׁוְּעֵנוּ אֵלֶיךָ
בְּנָשְׂאֵנוּ יָדֵינוּ אֶל־דְּבִיר קָדְשֶׁךָ.
שְׁמַע יהוה קוֹלֵנוּ נִקְרָא, חָנֵּנוּ וַעֲנֵנוּ.

תהלים פה
שׁוּבֵנוּ אֱלֹהֵי יִשְׁעֵנוּ, וְהָפֵר כַּעַסְךָ עִמָּנוּ:

ישעיה סד
אֵין קוֹרֵא בְשִׁמְךָ, מִתְעוֹרֵר לְהַחֲזִיק בָּךְ:

◂ שִׁמְעָה תְפִלָּתֵנוּ יהוה וְשַׁוְעָתֵנוּ הַאֲזִינָה, אֶל־דִּמְעָתֵנוּ אַל־תֶּחֱרַשׁ.

כְּרַחֵם אָב עַל־בָּנִים, כֵּן תְּרַחֵם יהוה עָלֵינוּ.

תהלים ג
לַיהוה הַיְשׁוּעָה, עַל־עַמְּךָ בִרְכָתֶךָ סֶּלָה:

תהלים מו
יהוה צְבָאוֹת עִמָּנוּ, מִשְׂגָּב לָנוּ אֱלֹהֵי יַעֲקֹב סֶלָה:

תהלים פד
יהוה צְבָאוֹת, אַשְׁרֵי אָדָם בֹּטֵחַ בָּךְ:

תהלים כ
יהוה הוֹשִׁיעָה, הַמֶּלֶךְ יַעֲנֵנוּ בְיוֹם־קָרְאֵנוּ:

במדבר יד
◂ סְלַח־נָא לַעֲוֹן הָעָם הַזֶּה כְּגֹדֶל חַסְדֶּךָ
וְכַאֲשֶׁר נָשָׂאתָה לָעָם הַזֶּה מִמִּצְרַיִם וְעַד־הֵנָּה:
וְשָׁם נֶאֱמַר

שליח ציבור then the קהל The:
וַיֹּאמֶר יהוה, סָלַחְתִּי כִּדְבָרֶךָ:

דניאל ט
הַטֵּה אֱלֹהַי אָזְנְךָ וּשֲׁמָע
פְּקַח עֵינֶיךָ וּרְאֵה שֹׁמְמֹתֵינוּ וְהָעִיר אֲשֶׁר־נִקְרָא שִׁמְךָ עָלֶיהָ
כִּי לֹא עַל־צִדְקֹתֵינוּ אֲנַחְנוּ מַפִּילִים תַּחֲנוּנֵינוּ לְפָנֶיךָ
כִּי עַל־רַחֲמֶיךָ הָרַבִּים:

---

sinner engages in sincere repentance the Almighty will erase any trace of sin from His memory.

בֹּקֶר, יהוה O Lord, at daybreak. Each one of the Seliḥot is preceded by a small selection of Scriptural verses which serve as a model for the prayer that

Master, hear me; Master, forgive;
Master, listen and act and do not delay –
➤ for Your sake, my God; for Your city and Your people bear Your name.

Our God and the God of our ancestors,

There is no one to call out in righteous prayer –
The best of men can be likened to thorny weeds.
There is no one to seek mercy
        for those who have been crushed –
No one worthy can be found.

The innocent and the pure are no more,
The pious are gone; the righteous have been trampled.
A meagre generation is caught out by its own offences,
Who can be found to show them the way?

Our sins have only kindled the wrath
Against those who offer themselves as advocates;
Is there anyone, great or small, who has the strength
To confess and pray before the Ever-Wakeful Holy One?

I am trembling and frightened to cry out
        for the sake of the camp,
To the One who probes and rakes hearts,
Devoid of virtue, brimming with sin,
How can I find grace through my supplication?

---

for forgiveness. We are sullied by sin, and our religious and moral integrity is inadequate to allow us to properly beseech Him for the pardon that we crave. So, we ask God to overlook our shortcomings and to imagine that we are worthy of petitioning Him, with the hope that He will not be dismissive of our earnest requests.

This *Seliḥa* is composed in verses of four rhyming stichs with a double-alphabetic acrostic – each one of the first two phrases begins with the letter *alef*, the next two phrases with the letter *bet*, and so on. It was authored by Rabbi Shlomo HaBavli, a prolific tenth-century composer of liturgical texts,

אֲדֹנָי שְׁמָעָה, אֲדֹנָי סְלָחָה
אֲדֹנָי הַקְשִׁיבָה וַעֲשֵׂה אַל תְּאַחַר
‹ לְמַעַנְךָ אֱלֹהַי כִּי־שִׁמְךָ נִקְרָא עַל־עִירְךָ וְעַל־עַמֶּךָ:

אֱלֹהֵינוּ וֵאלֹהֵי אֲבוֹתֵינוּ

אֵין מִי יִקְרָא בְּצֶדֶק
אִישׁ טוֹב נִמְשַׁל כְּחֶדֶק
בַּקֵּשׁ רַחֲמִים בְּעַד שְׁחוּקֵי הָדֶק
בְּשׁוּם פָּנִים אֵין בָּדֶק.

גֶּבֶר תָּמִים וְנָבָר אָפַס
גָּמַר חָסִיד וְצַדִּיק נִרְפָּשׂ
דּוֹר עָנִי בַּעֲוֹנוֹ נִתְפַּשׂ
דְּבָרָיו לְהַגִּיד מִי יַחְפֹּשׂ.

הוֹסַפְנוּ בַחֲטָאֵינוּ חֵמָה לְהַבְעִיר
הַמִּתְנַדְּבִים כִּבְנֵי בַיִת לְהַפְעִיר
וּמַה יַּעֲצֹר כֹּחַ רַב וְצָעִיר
וִדּוּי וּפָלֵל לְקָדִישׁ וָעִיר.

זָחַלְתִּי וָאִירָא בְּעַד מֵחָן
זַעַק לַחֲווֹת לְחוֹקֵר בְּבֹחַן
חָסַר חֶסֶד וְיִתּוּר צֶחָן
חֵן אֵיךְ אֶמְצָא בְּתָחַן.

אֵין מִי יִקְרָא *There is no one to call out.* This first formal *Seliḥa* of the night highlights the challenges inherent when trying to approach the Almighty

You are good to those who call out
.....to You with all their soul –
You bear their burden and grant their sustenance,
May You extend Your precious kindness to me;
May You give ear to my voice with love.

As one of worthy deeds, who prays wholeheartedly,
As one mature and fluent – not as a fool –
Consider my broken soul before You,
.....and let it not be shamed,
For the sake of my relief, recall Your mercy –
.....let it not be obscured.

Our needs are so many, but they cannot be expressed,
For we are too rash and too bitter;
But all is laid out before You, Who formed us from clay,
Lead us; guide us; shelter us; keep us!

We are left like a lone flagstone atop a hill in our solitude;
Swill and filth has replaced our glory.
Answer us; grant us satisfaction through servitude;
Count once more and seek out those
.....who have been lost to us.

Those suffering the pain of Your rod of reproach
Are scattered, dispersed, and pawned among the nations;
Conceal them in Your haven from trial and tribulation,
For all they hope is to gaze upon Your glory.

The force of Your voice hews flames of fire;
You mete out both good and its opposite.
Your beloved ones knock at Your door
.....with sounds of woe;
Accept the prayers they offer,
.....and take Your position among them.

---

who lived in Italy. His name is contained in an acrostic of the first letters of
the final four phrases of the *Seliḥa*.

טוֹב לְקוֹרְאֶיךָ בְּנֶפֶשׁ רָהָב
טָרָחָם נָשֹׁא וּלְכַלְכֵּל יָהָב
יָקַר חַסְדְּךָ עָלַי יִרְהָב
יַעַן קוֹלִי לְהַאֲזִין בְּאַהֲב.

כַּהֲגוֹן מִדּוֹת וּבִתְפִלָּה שָׁלֵם
כְּזָקֵן וְרָגִיל וְלֹא כְגֹלֶם
לְהֵחָשֵׁב נֶגְדְּךָ דִּכְאַי מִלְּהִכָּלֵם
לְרַחֲמֶיךָ זָכְרָה לְרַוְחָתִי מֵהִתְעַלֵּם.

מַרְבִּים צְרָכֵינוּ וְאֵין לְהֵאָמֵר
מִקֹּצֶר דֵּעָה וּמֵרֹב מֶמֶר
נֶגְדְּךָ הַכֹּל יוֹצֵר חֹמֶר
נוֹהֵג וְרוֹעֶה צֵל וְשׁוֹמֵר.

שָׁרַדְנוּ כְּתֹרֶן הַר בְּדוּדֵינוּ
סָחִי וּמָאוֹס הוּשַׂם כְּבוֹדֵנוּ
עֲנֵנוּ וּתְנֵנוּ מִחְיָה בְּשִׁעְבּוּדֵנוּ
עוֹד לְמַעַנְךָ בַּקֵּשׁ אֲבוּדֵינוּ.

פְּקֻדַּת נִגְעֵי תוֹכְחוֹתֶיךָ שְׁבוּטִים
פְּזוּרִים פְּרוּדִים וּבַגּוֹיִם עֲבוּטִים
צָפְנֵם בְּסֻכָּךְ מֵרִיב וּשְׁפָטִים
צְפִית תִּפְאַרְתָּךְ לֵמוֹ מַבָּטִים.

קוֹל כֹּחֲךָ לַהַב חוֹצֵב
קֶצֶב טוֹב וְחִלּוּפוֹ קוֹצֵב
רֵעֶיךָ דוֹפְקִים בְּקוֹל עָצֵב
רְצוֹת נִדְבָתָם וּבְקָרְבָּם הִתְיַצֵּב.

Those who persist in fasting to subdue their hearts
To save their masses from wrath –
    conceal them in Your inner chambers;
They move their lips in silent appeal
Please – do not withhold their desire!

‣ Your name, O God, revels in life,
Through You, we retain good life;
For the fountain of life wells forth from You.
Gaze down; answer us; light up our eyes!

אֵל מֶלֶךְ God, King who sits upon a throne of compassion, who acts
with loving-kindness, who pardons the iniquities of His people,
passing them before Him in order; who forgives sinners and pardons
transgressors; who performs righteousness with all flesh and spirit,
do not repay their bad actions in kind. ‣ God, You taught us to speak
thirteen attributes: recall for us today the covenant of the thirteen
attributes, as You in ancient times showed the humble one [Moses],
as is written: The Lord descended in the cloud and stood with him   *Ex. 34*
there, and proclaimed in the name of the Lord:

The congregation then the Leader:

וַיַּעֲבֹר And the Lord passed by before him and proclaimed: *Ibid.*

All say aloud:

יהוה The Lord, the Lord, compassionate and gracious God,
    slow to anger, abounding in loving-kindness and truth,
extending loving-kindness to a thousand generations, forgiving
iniquity, rebellion and sin, and absolving [the guilty who repent].

All continue:

Forgive us our iniquity and our sin,
and take us as Your inheritance.

סְלַח לָנוּ Forgive us, our Father, for we have sinned.
Pardon us, our King, for we have transgressed.
For You, Lord, are good and forgiving,   *Ps. 86*
abounding in loving-kindness to all who call on You.

שׁוֹקְדִים בְּצוֹם לְבָם לְהַכְנִיעַ
שְׁאוֹנָם מִזֶּעַם בַּחֲדָרֶיךָ תַּצְנִיעַ
תּוֹבְעִים בְּלַחַשׁ שָׂפָה לְהָנִיעַ
תַּאֲוָתָם אַל נָא תַּמְנִיעַ.

‹ שִׁמְךָ אֱלֹהִים חַיִּים מִתְפָּאֵר
וּלְחַיִּים טוֹבִים מִמְּךָ נִשְׁאָר
מְקוֹר חַיִּים עִמְּךָ מִתְבָּאֵר
הַבִּיטָה וַעֲנֵנוּ וְעֵינֵינוּ הָאֵר.

אֵל מֶלֶךְ יוֹשֵׁב עַל כִּסֵּא רַחֲמִים, מִתְנַהֵג בַּחֲסִידוּת. מוֹחֵל עֲוֹנוֹת
עַמּוֹ, מַעֲבִיר רִאשׁוֹן רִאשׁוֹן. מַרְבֶּה מְחִילָה לְחַטָּאִים, וּסְלִיחָה
לְפוֹשְׁעִים. עֹשֶׂה צְדָקוֹת עִם כָּל בָּשָׂר וָרוּחַ, לֹא כְרָעָתָם תִּגְמֹל.
‹ אֵל, הוֹרֵיתָ לָנוּ לוֹמַר שְׁלֹשׁ עֶשְׂרֵה, זְכֹר לָנוּ הַיּוֹם בְּרִית שְׁלֹשׁ
עֶשְׂרֵה, כְּמוֹ שֶׁהוֹדַעְתָּ לֶעָנָו מִקֶּדֶם, כְּמוֹ שֶׁכָּתוּב: וַיֵּרֶד יהוה שמות לד
בֶּעָנָן, וַיִּתְיַצֵּב עִמּוֹ שָׁם, וַיִּקְרָא בְשֵׁם יהוה:

שליח ציבור then the קהל The:

וַיַּעֲבֹר יהוה עַל־פָּנָיו וַיִּקְרָא שם

All say aloud:

יהוה, יהוה, אֵל רַחוּם וְחַנּוּן, אֶרֶךְ אַפַּיִם, וְרַב־חֶסֶד וֶאֱמֶת:
נֹצֵר חֶסֶד לָאֲלָפִים, נֹשֵׂא עָוֹן וָפֶשַׁע וְחַטָּאָה, וְנַקֵּה:

All continue:

וְסָלַחְתָּ לַעֲוֹנֵנוּ וּלְחַטָּאתֵנוּ וּנְחַלְתָּנוּ:

סְלַח לָנוּ, אָבִינוּ, כִּי חָטָאנוּ. מְחַל לָנוּ, מַלְכֵּנוּ, כִּי פָשָׁעְנוּ.
כִּי־אַתָּה, יהוה, טוֹב וְסַלָּח וְרַב־חֶסֶד לְכָל־קֹרְאֶיךָ: תהלים פו

מִקְוֵה יִשְׂרָאֵל Hope of Israel, its Saviour in times of trouble,   *Jer. 14*
Why should You be like a person stunned,
like a warrior unable to rescue?
‣ Arise and come to our aid, and redeem us   *Ps. 44*
for the sake of Your loving-kindness.

כְּרַחֵם As a father has compassion for his children,
so, Lord, have compassion for us.
Salvation belongs to the Lord;   *Ps. 3*
may Your blessing rest upon Your people, Selah!
The Lord of hosts is with us,   *Ps. 46*
the God of Jacob is our stronghold, Selah!
Lord of hosts: happy is the one who trusts in You.   *Ps. 84*
Lord, save! May the King answer us on the day we call.   *Ps. 20*

‣ סְלַח־נָא Forgive, please, this people's iniquity,   *Num. 14*
in the abundance of Your kindness,
and as You have forgiven this people
from the time of Egypt until now,
and there it is said:

Congregation then the Leader:
And the Lord said, I have forgiven as you asked.

הַטֵּה Give ear, my God and hear;   *Dan. 9*
open Your eyes and see our desolation,
and the city that bears Your name,
for it is not on the strength of our righteousness
that we throw down our pleadings before You,
but on the strength of Your great compassion.
Master, hear me;
Master, forgive;
Master, listen and act and do not delay –
‣ for Your sake, my God; for Your city
and Your people bear Your name.

מִקְוֵה יִשְׂרָאֵל יהוה, מוֹשִׁיעוֹ בְּעֵת צָרָה:

לָמָּה תִהְיֶה כְּאִישׁ נִדְהָם כְּגִבּוֹר לֹא־יוּכַל לְהוֹשִׁיעַ:

‹ קוּמָה עֶזְרָתָה לָּנוּ, וּפְדֵנוּ לְמַעַן חַסְדֶּךָ:

כְּרַחֵם אָב עַל בָּנִים, כֵּן תְּרַחֵם יהוה עָלֵינוּ.

לַיהוה הַיְשׁוּעָה, עַל־עַמְּךָ בִרְכָתֶךָ סֶּלָה:

יהוה צְבָאוֹת עִמָּנוּ, מִשְׂגָּב לָנוּ אֱלֹהֵי יַעֲקֹב סֶלָה:

יהוה צְבָאוֹת, אַשְׁרֵי אָדָם בֹּטֵחַ בָּךְ:

יהוה הוֹשִׁיעָה, הַמֶּלֶךְ יַעֲנֵנוּ בְיוֹם־קָרְאֵנוּ:

‹ סְלַח־נָא לַעֲוֹן הָעָם הַזֶּה כְּגֹדֶל חַסְדֶּךָ

וְכַאֲשֶׁר נָשָׂאתָה לָעָם הַזֶּה מִמִּצְרַיִם וְעַד־הֵנָּה:

וְשָׁם נֶאֱמַר

The קהל *then the* שליח ציבור:

וַיֹּאמֶר יהוה, סָלַחְתִּי כִּדְבָרֶךָ:

הַטֵּה אֱלֹהַי אָזְנְךָ וּשֲׁמָע

פְּקַח עֵינֶיךָ וּרְאֵה שֹׁמְמֹתֵינוּ

וְהָעִיר אֲשֶׁר־נִקְרָא שִׁמְךָ עָלֶיהָ

כִּי לֹא עַל־צִדְקֹתֵינוּ אֲנַחְנוּ מַפִּילִים תַּחֲנוּנֵינוּ לְפָנֶיךָ

כִּי עַל־רַחֲמֶיךָ הָרַבִּים:

אֲדֹנָי שְׁמָעָה

אֲדֹנָי סְלָחָה

אֲדֹנָי הַקְשִׁיבָה וַעֲשֵׂה אַל תְּאַחַר

‹ לְמַעַנְךָ אֱלֹהַי כִּי־שִׁמְךָ נִקְרָא עַל־עִירְךָ וְעַל־עַמֶּךָ:

ירמיה יד

תהלים מד

תהלים ג

תהלים מו

תהלים פד

תהלים כ

במדבר יד

דניאל ט

Our God and the God of our ancestors,

Though our faults have greatly increased,
like thick twisted ropes testifying against us,
parting us from You,
let Your merciful ways not cease.

Act through the attribute of Kindness, as You pledged,
O Never-Changing One,
remember the congregation You produced;
acquit the remnants of the one You called Your firstborn.

You raised us up; we were perched atop the highest heights,
we dwelled upon clifftops in all our might.
But all at once, You brought us crashing down
     to where jackals roam.
How long must we wait for our relief?

Shaken by terror and panic,
my soul sinks to the dust in loathing,
crawling and grovelling along the ground;
awake, O Hope, why do You sleep?

Open the prison willingly; declare freedom
     for Your captives;
hasten the end of these troubled times.
Gather in Your dispersed, Your scattered flock,
look upon the evil and clamp its mouth shut.

---

caused a gulf to develop between us and Him. Like many of the *Seliḥot*, it explains that the suffering of the Jewish people in exile is a punishment for our sinfulness, and it describes the dispersion of the Jewish nation in grim terms.

The *tokheḥa* (reproof) that appears at the end of the book of Leviticus (26:14–46) concludes with a promise that, despite all the suffering that the Jewish people might endure, having strayed from the laws of the Torah, God will always remember the covenant that He established with Abraham, Isaac and Jacob. This covenant, and the concept of *zekhut avot*, through which we can be redeemed thanks to the merit of our forebears, appears repeatedly

אֱלֹהֵינוּ וֵאלֹהֵי אֲבוֹתֵינוּ

אִם עֲוֹנֵנוּ רַבּוּ לְהַגְדִּיל
בָּנוּ עָנוּ עֲבוֹת כַּגְדִיל
גָּרְמוּ לָנוּ בְּנָתֵים לְהַבְדִּיל
דַּרְכֵי רַחֲמֶיךָ לֹא תַחְדִּיל.

הִתְנַהֵג בְּמִדַּת חֶסֶד הִתְנֵיתָ
וְאַתָּה הוּא לֹא שָׁנֵיתָ
זְכֹר עֲדָתְךָ אֲשֶׁר קָנֵיתָ
חֹן שִׁירֵי בְכוֹר כִּנֵּיתָ.

טְעַנְתָּנוּ גַּפֵּי קֶרֶת נְתוּנִים
יְשַׁבְתָּנוּ שֵׁן סֶלַע אֵיתָנִים
כְּאַחַת דְּכִיתָנוּ בִּמְקוֹם תַּנִּים
לְרַוְיָה צֵאת כַּמָּה מְתוּנִים.

מֵרֹב פְּקֻדּוֹת וּבֶהָלָה מְחַלְחֶלֶת
נִקְטָה שָׁחָה נַפְשִׁי, לֶעָפָר בּוֹחֶלֶת
סָמְכָה בֶטֶן לָאָרֶץ, נִשְׁחֶלֶת
עוּרָה, לָמָּה תִישַׁן, תּוֹחֶלֶת.

פְּקַח קֹוחַ קְרָא אֲסוּרֶיךָ חֲפֹץ
צוֹק הָעִתִּים חֶשְׁבּוֹנָם קְפֹץ
קַבֵּץ פְּזוּרֶיךָ עֵדֶר הַנָּפֹץ
רְאוֹת עֹלָתָהּ פִּיהָ תִּקְפֹּץ.

___

אִם עֲוֹנֵנוּ *Though our faults.* This *Seliḥa,* which appears elsewhere as a *Seliḥa*
for the second day, asks God to forgive us despite the fact that our sins have

Keep the promise of loyalty You swore
to the mild [Jacob], to he whose ashes would
     have heaped upon the altar[Isaac],
     and to the builder [Abraham], our mighty ancestors.
Let Him command His peace to end our condemnation,
revert and change this age for the better.

▸ Though Jacob is small and feeble,
well acquainted with suffering, despised and shunned,
grant him life and kindness, O Tower of Strength.
Now, as of old, let Your power increase!

אֵל מֶלֶךְ God, King who sits upon a throne of compassion, who acts with loving-kindness, who pardons the iniquities of His people, passing them before Him in order; who forgives sinners and pardons transgressors; who performs righteousness with all flesh and spirit, do not repay their bad actions in kind. ▸ God, You taught us to speak thirteen attributes: recall for us today the covenant of the thirteen attributes, as You in ancient times showed the humble one [Moses], as is written: The Lord descended in the cloud and stood with him there, and proclaimed in the name of the Lord: *Ex. 34*

The congregation then the Leader:
וַיַּעֲבֹר And the Lord passed by before him and proclaimed: *Ibid.*

All say aloud:
יהוה The Lord, the Lord, compassionate and gracious God,
     slow to anger, abounding in loving-kindness and truth,
extending loving-kindness to a thousand generations, forgiving
iniquity, rebellion and sin, and absolving [the guilty who repent].

All continue:
Forgive us our iniquity and our sin, and take us as Your inheritance.

Ta'anit 2:1); and בַּנַּאי – the builder (i.e., Abraham, who built an altar to God – Genesis 12:8).

Like the previous *Seliḥa*, "*Im Avoneinu*" was also composed by Rabbi Shlomo HaBavli (referred to by Rashi in his commentary to the Ḥumash as "the Babylonian") and takes the form of an alphabetic acrostic with verses of four rhyming stichs.

שָׁמוֹ שְׁבוּעַת חֶסֶד וּתְנָאִי

תָּם וְצָבוּר וּבַנַּאי אִיתְּנֵי

שְׁלוֹמוֹ יְצַוֶּה בְּלִי גְנַאי

הֲפֹךְ וְשַׁנּוֹת לְטוֹבָה הַפְנָאִי.

‹ קָטֹן כִּי יַעֲקֹב וְדַל

יָדוּעַ חֳלִי נִבְזֶה וַחֲדָל

חַיִּים וָחֶסֶד, מָעוֹז וּמִגְדָּל

כַּאֲשֶׁר כֹּחֲךָ עַתָּה יִגְדָּל.

אֵל מֶלֶךְ יוֹשֵׁב עַל כִּסֵּא רַחֲמִים, מִתְנַהֵג בַּחֲסִידוּת. מוֹחֵל עֲוֹנוֹת עַמּוֹ, מַעֲבִיר רִאשׁוֹן רִאשׁוֹן. מַרְבֶּה מְחִילָה לַחַטָּאִים, וּסְלִיחָה לַפּוֹשְׁעִים. עוֹשֶׂה צְדָקוֹת עִם כָּל בָּשָׂר וָרוּחַ, לֹא כְרָעָתָם תִּגְמֹל. ‹ אֵל, הוֹרֵיתָ לָנוּ לוֹמַר שְׁלֹשׁ עֶשְׂרֵה, זְכֹר לָנוּ הַיּוֹם בְּרִית שְׁלֹשׁ עֶשְׂרֵה, כְּמוֹ שֶׁהוֹדַעְתָּ לֶעָנָו מִקֶּדֶם, כְּמוֹ שֶׁכָּתוּב: וַיֵּרֶד יהוה בֶּעָנָן, וַיִּתְיַצֵּב עִמּוֹ שָׁם, וַיִּקְרָא בְשֵׁם יהוה: שמות לד

שם

The קהל *then the* שליח ציבור:

וַיַּעֲבֹר יהוה עַל־פָּנָיו וַיִּקְרָא

All say aloud:

יהוה, יהוה, אֵל רַחוּם וְחַנּוּן, אֶרֶךְ אַפַּיִם, וְרַב־חֶסֶד וֶאֱמֶת: נֹצֵר חֶסֶד לָאֲלָפִים, נֹשֵׂא עָוֹן וָפֶשַׁע וְחַטָּאָה, וְנַקֵּה:

All continue:

וְסָלַחְתָּ לַעֲוֹנֵנוּ וּלְחַטָּאתֵנוּ וּנְחַלְתָּנוּ:

in the *Seliḥot*. The three patriarchs are referenced at the end of this *Seliḥa* as "תָּם וְצָבוּר וּבַנַּאי". תָּם, meaning mild or pure, refers to Jacob (described in the Torah as אִישׁ תָּם, a pure-hearted person – Genesis 25:27); צָבוּר means the one who is heaped (that is, Isaac: according to rabbinic tradition, his ashes were gathered upon the altar at the time of the *Akeida* – Yerushalmi

סְלַח לָֽנוּ Forgive us, our Father, for we have sinned.
Pardon us, our King, for we have transgressed.
For You, LORD, are good and forgiving,   *Ps. 86*
abounding in loving-kindness to all who call on You.

תָּבוֹא Let our prayer come before You,
and do not hide Yourself from our plea.
Let our prayer come before You, to Your holy Sanctuary.
Let a prisoner's cry come to You; and as accords to Your arm's great   *Ps. 79*
power – release these people bound to die.
‣ Our God, we are humiliated by our actions, ashamed of our sins.

כְּרַחֵם As a father has compassion for his children,
so, LORD, have compassion for us.
Salvation belongs to the LORD;   *Ps. 3*
may Your blessing rest upon Your people, Selah!
The LORD of hosts is with us,   *Ps. 46*
the God of Jacob is our stronghold, Selah!
LORD of hosts: happy is the one who trusts in You.   *Ps. 84*
LORD, save! May the King answer us on the day we call.   *Ps. 20*

> ‣ סְלַח־נָא Forgive, please, this people's iniquity,   *Num. 14*
> in the abundance of Your kindness,
> and as You have forgiven this people
> from the time of Egypt until now,
> and there it is said:

Congregation then the Leader:
And the LORD said, I have forgiven as you asked.

הַטֵּה Give ear, my God and hear;   *Dan. 9*
open Your eyes and see our desolation, and the city that bears Your name,
for it is not on the strength of our righteousness
that we throw down our pleadings before You,
but on the strength of Your great compassion.
Master, hear me; Master, forgive;
Master, listen and act and do not delay –
‣ for Your sake, my God; for Your city and Your people bear Your name.

סְלַח לָנוּ, אָבִינוּ, כִּי חָטָאנוּ. מְחַל לָנוּ, מַלְכֵּנוּ, כִּי פָשָׁעְנוּ.
כִּי־אַתָּה, יהוה, טוֹב וְסַלָּח וְרַב־חֶסֶד לְכָל־קֹרְאֶיךָ:

תָּבוֹא לְפָנֶיךָ תְּפִלָּתֵנוּ וְאַל תִּתְעַלַּם מִתְּחִנָּתֵנוּ.
תָּבוֹא לְפָנֶיךָ תְּפִלָּתֵנוּ אֶל הֵיכַל קָדְשֶׁךָ.
תָּבוֹא לְפָנֶיךָ אֶנְקַת אָסִיר, כְּגֹדֶל זְרוֹעֲךָ הוֹתֵר בְּנֵי־תְמוּתָה:
‹ אֱלֹהֵינוּ, בֹּשְׁנוּ בְּמַעֲשֵׂינוּ וְנִכְלַמְנוּ בַּעֲוֹנֵינוּ.

כְּרַחֵם אָב עַל בָּנִים, כֵּן תְּרַחֵם יהוה עָלֵינוּ.
לַיהוה הַיְשׁוּעָה, עַל־עַמְּךָ בִרְכָתֶךָ סֶּלָה:
יהוה צְבָאוֹת עִמָּנוּ, מִשְׂגָּב לָנוּ אֱלֹהֵי יַעֲקֹב סֶלָה:
יהוה צְבָאוֹת, אַשְׁרֵי אָדָם בֹּטֵחַ בָּךְ:
יהוה הוֹשִׁיעָה, הַמֶּלֶךְ יַעֲנֵנוּ בְיוֹם־קָרְאֵנוּ:

תהלים פו
תהלים עט
תהלים ג
תהלים מו
תהלים פד
תהלים כ

‹ סְלַח־נָא לַעֲוֹן הָעָם הַזֶּה כְּגֹדֶל חַסְדֶּךָ
וְכַאֲשֶׁר נָשָׂאתָה לָעָם הַזֶּה מִמִּצְרַיִם וְעַד־הֵנָּה:
וְשָׁם נֶאֱמַר

במדבר יד

The קהל then the שליח ציבור:
וַיֹּאמֶר יהוה, סָלַחְתִּי כִּדְבָרֶךָ:

הַטֵּה אֱלֹהַי אָזְנְךָ וּשֲׁמָע
פְּקַח עֵינֶיךָ וּרְאֵה שֹׁמְמֹתֵינוּ וְהָעִיר אֲשֶׁר־נִקְרָא שִׁמְךָ עָלֶיהָ
כִּי לֹא עַל־צִדְקֹתֵינוּ אֲנַחְנוּ מַפִּילִים תַּחֲנוּנֵינוּ לְפָנֶיךָ
כִּי עַל־רַחֲמֶיךָ הָרַבִּים:
אֲדֹנָי שְׁמָעָה, אֲדֹנָי סְלָחָה
אֲדֹנָי הַקְשִׁיבָה וַעֲשֵׂה אַל־תְּאַחַר
‹ לְמַעַנְךָ אֱלֹהַי כִּי־שִׁמְךָ נִקְרָא עַל־עִירְךָ וְעַל־עַמֶּךָ:

דניאל ט

Our God and the God of our ancestors,

May our fervent pleas come before You,
may Your ear be attuned to our supplication.
Hear our justification, O LORD, listen to our chant,
see our rectitude, overlook rants against us.

We are too ashamed, too disgraced
      to raise our heads,
for the scent of our good deeds now reeks.
We have ruined virtue, and corrupted the Torah;
hence we bury our faces in the ground.

Stress and strife on every side,
we drift like sheep without shelter.
If we turn to the right, the axe cuts us down;
on the left is terror – of falling prey to the hunter.

May Your ever-seeing eyes be open
to our drawn-out trials and tribulations.
May our grief turn to joy, to approval reproof;
reverse our misfortunes in Your upright ways.

Our sins have subjected us to capture and plunder,
we, our kings, our priests, to disgrace.
From the heights of glory and fierce love,
You have hurled us to the earth
      in desolation and scorn.

---

the double alphabetic acrostic is slightly more complex, working backwards
from *tav* to *alef*, followed by an acrostic of the author's name. Like the pre-
ceding *Seliḥa*, this composition laments the suffering of the Jewish people in
their dispersion as a punishment for the sins which caused the destruction
of the Temple and the subsequent exile. In a style which is characteristic of
Seliḥot and other liturgical compositions, many of the phrases of this passage
allude to or adapt biblical verses. A familiarity with Midrashic imagery is
required to fully understand the meanings of some of the expressions. For
example, this *Seliḥa* refers to "בְּשַׁפַּל קוֹל הַטַּחֲנָה", When we stooped to stifle the

אֱלֹהֵינוּ וֵאלֹהֵי אֲבוֹתֵינוּ

תָּבֹא לְפָנֶיךָ שַׁוְעַת חִנּוּן
תְּהִי נָא אָזְנְךָ קַשֶּׁבֶת תַּחֲנוּן
שִׁמְעָה יהוה צֶדֶק, הַקְשִׁיבָה רִנּוּן
שָׂר מֵישָׁרִים וּמַעֲלִים מֵרְנוּן.

רֹאשׁ לְהָרִים נִכְלַמְנוּ בְּשָׁנוּ
רֵיחַ נִרְדֵּנוּ כִּי הִבְאַשְׁנוּ
קִלְקַלְנוּ יְשָׁרִים וְתוֹרוֹת שִׁבַּשְׁנוּ
קַרְקַע פָּנֵינוּ בְּכֵן כָּבָשְׁנוּ.

צַר וּמָצוֹק מִכָּל צַד
צֹאן נִדָּחָה מֵאֵין מָצֵד
פָּנָה לְיָמִין וַיִּגְזֹר מַעֲצָד
פַּחַד מִשְּׂמֹאל וְצַיִד הַצָּד.

עֵינֶיךָ רֹאוֹת תִּהְיֶינָה פְּקֻחוֹת
עֳנִי וְעִנּוּי מִצָּרוֹת הַמְּתוּחוֹת
סְפֹד לְרָנָּה וּלְרָצוֹי תּוֹכָחוֹת
סַבּוֹת וַהֲפֹךְ בְּדָרְכֶיךָ הַנְּכוֹחוֹת.

נִתְּנוּ בַעֲוֹנֵינוּ לְשֶׁבִי וּלְבִזָּה
נֶחְנוּ מַלְכֵּינוּ כְּהֶגְיֵנוּ לְבוּזָה
מָרוֹם נִכְבָּדוֹת וְאַהֲבָה עַזָּה
מְגֹרַת לָאָרֶץ לְשַׁמָּה וּלְעֻזָּה.

תָּבֹא לְפָנֶיךָ שַׁוְעַת חִנּוּן *May our fervent pleas come before You.* The third *Seliḥa* of this service is also a composition of Rabbi Shlomo HaBavli. In this instance,

We failed to seek Your presence to offer supplication,
nor did we contemplate Your truths,
because of the stench of our sins.
We would have perished like Sodom
when we stooped to stifle the sound of Torah,
on the brink of destruction – but for Your grace.

You spared the remnant of the First Temple,
You secured, fenced, and gathered us in to the Second.
But You flung us around because of three despised sins,
and trampled a Temple of yearning because of us.

Our acts of corruption and violation
drove us from yoke to yoke.
Recall how You committed not to abhor us;
gather Your scattered and rule over them.

After all that has befallen us,
You are certain and just, while we are in disgrace.
To this very day we have not turned around;
here we are before You in grave guilt.

The lowliest of people, held in shame and contempt,
ravaged, savaged, swept away,
tested and purged through exile and enslavement;
reverse them, in kindness, to pardon and cure.

Through Your recurring mercy,
may we be saved; fulfil the promise of "I will save them!"
Let them come thronging from afar,
from the north and from ships from Kittim.

---

sound of Torah" – the literal translation of which is "the sound of the mill."
This expression is a citation from the book of Ecclesiastes (12:4), which
the *Midrash Raba* interprets as an allusion to *bitul Torah*, that is, wasteful-
ness with regard to Torah study. Just as the millstones in a busy mill never
cease turning, the sound of Torah study should never cease to be heard in
Jewish communities.

לֹא חִלִּינוּ פָנֶיךָ לְהַפִּיל תְּחִנָּה
לְהַשְׂכִּיל בַּאֲמִתְּךָ מֵעֲלוֹת צְחַנָּה
כָּלִּינוּ כִסְדוֹם בְּשֵׁפֶל קוֹל הַטְּחַנָּה
כִּמְעַט רֶגַע לוּלֵי תְחִנָּה.

יֶתֶר הַפְּלֵטָה לְהַשְׁאִיר חָסֶתָּ
יָתֵד וְגָדֵר תַּתָּה וְכָנַסְתָּ
טִלְטַלְתָּנוּ כְּנֶגֶד שָׁלֹשׁ מָאַסְתָּ
טִירַת כֶּסֶף בְּגַלְלֵנוּ רָמַסְתָּ.

חָבֹל חָבַלְנוּ מַעַל לְמַעַל
חִבַּלְנוּ מַעַל אֶל עַל
זְכֹר צִוִּיתָ בְּלִי לְגָעַל
זְרוּיִים לְקַבֵּץ וּבָם לִבְעַל.

וְאַתָּה, אַחֲרֵי כָּל הַבָּא
וַדַּאי וְצַדִּיק, וְלָנוּ הַדִּבָּה
הַיּוֹם כְּמֵאָז בְּלִי סִבָּה
הִנְנוּ לְפָנֶיךָ בְּאַשְׁמָה רַבָּה.

דַּלַּת עַם לְקֶלֶס וְחֵרוּף
דְּחוּפִים סְחוּפִים נְתוּנִים לְטֵרוּף
גָּלוּת וְשִׁעְבּוּד בְּנִסָּיוֹן וְצֵרוּף
גַּלְגֵּל בְּחֶסֶד לִסְלִיחָה וְתֵרוּף.

בְּרַחֲמֶיךָ עוֹד בִּרְבוֹת עִתִּים
בָּךְ נָשַׁע קַיֵּם וְהוֹשַׁעְתִּים
אֵלֶּה מֵרָחוֹק יָבֹאוּ כְּתִים
אֵלֶּה מִצָּפוֹן וּמִצִּים וְכֻתִּים.

They are Yours, Your servants and Your people;
cherish Your sweet ones as You did in times past.
Draw us after You; place us among Your listed ones,
for we all yearn to revere Your name.

‣ May this small people increase a thousandfold,
    our Merciful One,
And may these young ones become a mighty nation
    within our borders.
Together, through all Your righteous ways,
    have mercy upon us –
turn back from Your wrath, and comfort us.

אֵל מֶלֶךְ God, King who sits upon a throne of compassion, who acts with loving-kindness, who pardons the iniquities of His people, passing them before Him in order; who forgives sinners and pardons transgressors; who performs righteousness with all flesh and spirit, do not repay their bad actions in kind. ‣ God, You taught us to speak thirteen attributes: recall for us today the covenant of the thirteen attributes, as You in ancient times showed the humble one [Moses], as is written: The LORD descended in the cloud and stood with him *Ex. 34* there, and proclaimed in the name of the LORD:

The congregation then the Leader:

וַיַּעֲבֹר And the LORD passed by before him and proclaimed: *Ibid.*

All say aloud:

יהוה The LORD, the LORD, compassionate and gracious God,
    slow to anger, abounding in loving-kindness and truth,
extending loving-kindness to a thousand generations, forgiving
iniquity, rebellion and sin, and absolving [the guilty who repent].

All continue:

Forgive us our iniquity and our sin, and take us as Your inheritance.

סְלַח לָנוּ Forgive us, our Father, for we have sinned.
Pardon us, our King, for we have transgressed.
‣ For You, LORD, are good and forgiving,   *Ps. 86*
    abounding in loving-kindness to all who call on You.

שֶׁלְּךָ הֵם עֲבָדֶיךָ וְעַמֶּךָ
לְבַב כִּימֵי קֶדֶם נְעִימֶיךָ
מִשְׁכְּנוּ אַחֲרֶיךָ, שִׂימֵנוּ בִּרְשׁוּמֶיךָ
הַכֹּל חֲפֵצִים לְיִרְאָה אֶת שְׁמֶךָ.

‹ הַקָּטֹן לָאֶלֶף גַּדֵּל, רַחוּמֵנוּ
וְהַצָּעִיר לְגוֹי לְהַעֲצִים בְּתַחוּמֵנוּ
יַחַד בְּכָל צִדְקוֹתֶיךָ לְרַחֲמֵנוּ
יָשֹׁב נָא אַפְּךָ וּתְנַחֲמֵנוּ.

אֵל מֶלֶךְ יוֹשֵׁב עַל כִּסֵּא רַחֲמִים, מִתְנַהֵג בַּחֲסִידוּת. מוֹחֵל עֲוֹנוֹת
עַמּוֹ, מַעֲבִיר רִאשׁוֹן רִאשׁוֹן. מַרְבֶּה מְחִילָה לְחַטָּאִים, וּסְלִיחָה
לְפוֹשְׁעִים. עֹשֶׂה צְדָקוֹת עִם כָּל בָּשָׂר וָרוּחַ, לֹא כְרָעָתָם תִּגְמֹל.
‹ אֵל, הוֹרֵיתָ לָּנוּ לוֹמַר שְׁלֹשׁ עֶשְׂרֵה, וּזְכָר לָנוּ הַיּוֹם בְּרִית שְׁלֹשׁ
עֶשְׂרֵה, כְּהוֹדַעְתָּ לֶעָנָו מִקֶּדֶם, כְּמוֹ שֶׁכָּתוּב, וַיֵּרֶד יהוה בֶּעָנָן, שמות לד
וַיִּתְיַצֵּב עִמּוֹ שָׁם, וַיִּקְרָא בְשֵׁם יהוה:

שליח ציבור then the *קהל The*:

וַיַּעֲבֹר יהוה עַל־פָּנָיו וַיִּקְרָא

All say aloud:

יהוה, יהוה, אֵל רַחוּם וְחַנּוּן, אֶרֶךְ אַפַּיִם, וְרַב־חֶסֶד וֶאֱמֶת:
נֹצֵר חֶסֶד לָאֲלָפִים, נֹשֵׂא עָוֹן וָפֶשַׁע וְחַטָּאָה, וְנַקֵּה:

All continue:

וְסָלַחְתָּ לַעֲוֹנֵנוּ וּלְחַטָּאתֵנוּ וּנְחַלְתָּנוּ:

סְלַח לָנוּ, אָבִינוּ, כִּי חָטָאנוּ.
מְחַל לָנוּ, מַלְכֵּנוּ, כִּי פָשָׁעְנוּ.
‹ כִּי־אַתָּה, יהוה, טוֹב וְסַלָּח וְרַב־חֶסֶד לְכָל־קֹרְאֶיךָ: תהלים פו

The Ark is opened.

After the Day of Rest has departed, we first approach You.
Incline Your ear from on high, O One enthroned upon praise –
Hear our cry, and our prayer!

1 Kings 8

Raise up Your mighty right hand in valiance,
for the sake of the bound-up righteous one,
    in whose stead a ram was slain.
Shield his line, as they cry out while it is yet night –
        Hear our cry, and our prayer!

Seek out, now, those who seek You, as they seek Your presence,
Crave their prayers from Your heavenly abode,
Do not close Your ears to the pleas of their supplication –
        Hear our cry, and our prayer!

Trembling and shuddering at the day of Your coming,
they shake at the fury You bear like a woman
    giving birth to her first child.
Wipe away their filth now, so they may praise Your wonder –
        Hear our cry, and our prayer!

You are the Creator of every creature created;
long before creation, You planned the salve for their salvation,
and to grant them amnesty from Your reserved treasury –
        Hear our cry, and our prayer!

The refrain in this *pizmon*, "לִשְׁמֹעַ אֶל־הָרִנָּה וְאֶל־הַתְּפִלָּה, Hear our cry and our prayer," is taken from the prayer of King Solomon when he dedicated the Temple in Jerusalem (1 Kings 8:28). The classical commentators explain that רנה is the song of praise to God that must always precede our prayers to Him. This is an accurate description of the structure of the *Seliḥot* service thus far.

The fifth stanza in the *pizmon* states "כּוֹנַנְתָּ מֵאָז תֶּרֶף, Long before creation, You planned the salve" – God prepared a remedy for exile and dispersion long ago. This is a reference to the Talmudic assertion (*Pesaḥim* 54a) that repentance (described here as a remedy) was created by God before He formed the world. Knowing that people would have the capacity to sin, God ensured from the very outset that there would be a way for us to return to Him and to repair our fractured souls.

מלכים א׳ ח

The ארון קודש *is opened.*

בְּמוֹצָאֵי מְנוּחָה קִדַּמְנוּךְ תְּחִלָּה
הַט אָזְנְךָ מִמָּרוֹם, יוֹשֵׁב תְּהִלָּה
לִשְׁמֹעַ אֶל־הָרִנָּה וְאֶל־הַתְּפִלָּה:

אֶת יְמִין עֹז עוֹרְרָה לַעֲשׂוֹת חָיִל
בְּצֶדֶק נֶעֱקַד וְנִשְׁחַט תְּמוּרוֹ אַיִל
גְּנָן נָא גְּזָעוֹ בְּזַעֲקָם בְּעוֹד לַיִל
לִשְׁמֹעַ אֶל־הָרִנָּה וְאֶל־הַתְּפִלָּה:

דְּרֹשׁ נָא דוֹרְשֶׁיךָ בְּדָרְשָׁם פָּנֶיךָ
הִדָּרֶשׁ לָמוֹ מִשְּׁמֵי מְעוֹנֶךָ
וּלְשַׁוְעַת חֲנוּנָם אַל תַּעְלֵם אָזְנֶךָ
לִשְׁמֹעַ אֶל־הָרִנָּה וְאֶל־הַתְּפִלָּה:

זוֹחֲלִים וְרוֹעֲדִים מִיּוֹם בּוֹאֶךָ
חָלִים כְּמַבְכִּירָה מֵעֶבְרַת מַשָּׁאֶיךָ
טְנוּפָם מְחֵה נָא וְיוֹדוּ פְלָאֶיךָ
לִשְׁמֹעַ אֶל־הָרִנָּה וְאֶל־הַתְּפִלָּה:

יוֹצֵר אַתָּה לְכָל יְצִיר נוֹצָר
כּוֹנַנְתָּ מֵאָז טֶרֶף לְחַלְּצָם מִמַּעֲצָר
לְחָנְנָם חִנָּם מֵאוֹצָר הַמְּנֻצָּר
לִשְׁמֹעַ אֶל־הָרִנָּה וְאֶל־הַתְּפִלָּה:

בְּמוֹצָאֵי מְנוּחָה *After the Day of Rest has departed.* The *pizmon* (hymn with a chorus) is usually the poetic and liturgical centrepiece of each *Seliḥot* service and is recited responsively by the *ḥazan* and the congregation. This *pizmon* commences with a reference to the fact that the first *Seliḥot* are traditionally recited on Motza'ei Shabbat (or very early on Sunday morning). An introductory stanza is followed by verses of three rhyming phrases and a chorus, structured in an alphabetic acrostic, in common with so many of the *Seliḥot* and other *piyutim*.

Exalted One,
if Your congregation's crimes are too great,
raise us up with the treasure stored in Your heavenly skies.
Your community comes to You for undeserved grace –
Hear our cry, and our prayer!

Please turn to our troubles, but not to our sins;
acquit those who cry out to You, O Achiever of Wonders.
Please listen to their pleas, O God, LORD of hosts –
Hear our cry, and our prayer.

Find favour with the appeals of those who stand
before You by night;
accept them as willingly as the offering of sacrifices.
Show them Your miracles, He who does great things –
Hear our cry, and our prayer!

The Ark is closed.

אֵל מֶלֶךְ God, King who sits upon a throne of compassion, who acts
with loving-kindness, who pardons the iniquities of His people,
passing them before Him in order; who forgives sinners and pardons
transgressors; who performs righteousness with all flesh and spirit,
do not repay their bad actions in kind. ‣ God, You taught us to speak
thirteen attributes: recall for us today the covenant of the thirteen
attributes, as You in ancient times showed the humble one [Moses],
as is written: The LORD descended in the cloud and stood with him   *Ex. 34*
there, and proclaimed in the name of the LORD:

The congregation then the Leader:
וַיַּעֲבֹר And the LORD passed by before him and proclaimed: *Ibid.*

All say aloud:
יהוה The LORD, the LORD, compassionate and gracious God,
slow to anger, abounding in loving-kindness and truth,
extending loving-kindness to a thousand generations, forgiving
iniquity, rebellion and sin, and absolving [the guilty who repent].

All continue:
Forgive us our iniquity and our sin,
and take us as Your inheritance.

מָרוֹם, אִם עָצְמוּ פִּשְׁעֵי קְהָלֶךְ

נָא שַׂגְּבֵם מֵאוֹצַר הַמּוּכָן בִּזְבוּלֶךְ

עָדֶיךָ לָחֹן חִנָּם בָּאִים אֵלֶיךָ

לִשְׁמֹעַ אֶל־הָרִנָּה וְאֶל־הַתְּפִלָּה:

פְּנֵה נָא אֶל הַתְּלָאוֹת וְאַל לַחֲטָאוֹת

צַדֵּק צוֹעֲקֶיךָ, מַפְלִיא פְלָאוֹת

קְשָׁב נָא חִנּוּנָם, אֱלֹהִים יהוה צְבָאוֹת

לִשְׁמֹעַ אֶל־הָרִנָּה וְאֶל־הַתְּפִלָּה:

רְצֵה עֲתִירָתָם בְּעָמְדָם בַּלֵּילוֹת

שְׁעֵה נָא בְרָצוֹן כְּקָרְבָּן כָּלִיל וְעוֹלוֹת

תִּרְאֵם נִסֶּיךָ, עוֹשֵׂה גְדוֹלוֹת

לִשְׁמֹעַ אֶל־הָרִנָּה וְאֶל־הַתְּפִלָּה.

The ארון קודש *is closed.*

אֵל מֶלֶךְ יוֹשֵׁב עַל כִּסֵּא רַחֲמִים, מִתְנַהֵג בַּחֲסִידוּת. מוֹחֵל עֲוֹנוֹת
עַמּוֹ, מַעֲבִיר רִאשׁוֹן רִאשׁוֹן. מַרְבֶּה מְחִילָה לַחַטָּאִים, וּסְלִיחָה
לַפּוֹשְׁעִים. עוֹשֶׂה צְדָקוֹת עִם כָּל בָּשָׂר וָרוּחַ, לֹא כְרָעָתָם תִּגְמֹל.
‹ אֵל, הוֹרֵיתָ לָּנוּ לוֹמַר שְׁלֹשׁ עֶשְׂרֵה, וּזְכָר לָנוּ הַיּוֹם בְּרִית שְׁלֹשׁ
עֶשְׂרֵה, כְּהוֹדַעְתָּ לֶעָנָו מִקֶּדֶם, כְּמוֹ שֶׁכָּתוּב, וַיֵּרֶד יהוה בֶּעָנָן, שמות לד
וַיִּתְיַצֵּב עִמּוֹ שָׁם, וַיִּקְרָא בְשֵׁם יהוה:

The שליח ציבור *then the* קהל:

שם

וַיַּעֲבֹר יהוה עַל־פָּנָיו וַיִּקְרָא

All say aloud:

יהוה, יהוה, אֵל רַחוּם וְחַנּוּן, אֶרֶךְ אַפַּיִם, וְרַב־חֶסֶד וֶאֱמֶת:

נֹצֵר חֶסֶד לָאֲלָפִים, נֹשֵׂא עָוֹן וָפֶשַׁע וְחַטָּאָה, וְנַקֵּה:

All continue:

וְסָלַחְתָּ לַעֲוֹנֵנוּ וּלְחַטָּאתֵנוּ וּנְחַלְתָּנוּ:

סְלַח לָנוּ Forgive us, our Father, for we have sinned.
Pardon us, our King, for we have transgressed.
▸ For You, LORD, are good and forgiving,   *Ps. 86*
   abounding in loving-kindness to all who call on You.

זְכֹר Remember, LORD, Your compassion and loving-kindness,   *Ps. 25*
   for they are everlasting.
   Remember us, LORD, in favouring Your people;
   redeem us with Your salvation.
זְכֹר Remember Your congregation,   *Ps. 74*
   the one that You acquired long ago,
   the tribe of Your inheritance that You redeemed,
   this Mount Zion that You have dwelt in.
זְכֹר Remember, LORD, the fondness of Jerusalem;
   do not forever forget the love of Zion.
    You shall rise up and have compassion for Zion,   *Ps. 102*
   for now it is right to be gracious,
   for the time has come.
זְכֹר Remember, LORD, what the Edomites did   *Ps. 137*
   on the day Jerusalem fell.
   They said, "Tear it down, tear it down to its very foundations!"
זְכֹר Remember Abraham, Isaac and Yisrael, Your servants,   *Ex. 32*
   to whom You swore by Your own Self, when You said to them,
   "I shall make your descendants as numerous as the stars
   in the sky, and I shall give all this land that I spoke of to your
   descendants, and they shall inherit it forever."
זְכֹר Remember Your servants, Abraham, Isaac and Jacob;   *Deut. 9*
   do not attend to the stubbornness of this people,
   to their wickedness or sinfulness.

Leader:
אַל־נָא Please, do not hold against us the sin   *Num. 12*
   that we committed so foolishly, that we have sinned.

Congregation:
We have sinned, our Rock;
forgive us, our Creator.

סְלַח לָנוּ, אָבִינוּ, כִּי חָטָאנוּ.

מְחַל לָנוּ, מַלְכֵּנוּ, כִּי פָשָׁעְנוּ.

תהלים פו ‹ כִּי־אַתָּה, יהוה, טוֹב וְסַלָּח וְרַב־חֶסֶד לְכָל־קֹרְאֶיךָ:

תהלים כה זְכֹר־רַחֲמֶיךָ יהוה וַחֲסָדֶיךָ, כִּי מֵעוֹלָם הֵמָּה:

זָכְרֵנוּ יהוה בִּרְצוֹן עַמֶּךָ, פָּקְדֵנוּ בִּישׁוּעָתֶךָ.

תהלים עד זְכֹר עֲדָתְךָ קָנִיתָ קֶּדֶם, גָּאַלְתָּ שֵׁבֶט נַחֲלָתֶךָ

הַר־צִיּוֹן זֶה שָׁכַנְתָּ בּוֹ:

זְכֹר יהוה חִבַּת יְרוּשָׁלָיִם

אַהֲבַת צִיּוֹן אַל תִּשְׁכַּח לָנֶצַח.

תהלים קב אַתָּה תָקוּם תְּרַחֵם צִיּוֹן

כִּי־עֵת לְחֶנְנָהּ, כִּי־בָא מוֹעֵד:

תהלים קלז זְכֹר יהוה לִבְנֵי אֱדוֹם אֵת יוֹם יְרוּשָׁלָיִם

הָאוֹמְרִים עָרוּ עָרוּ, עַד הַיְסוֹד בָּהּ:

שמות לב זְכֹר לְאַבְרָהָם לְיִצְחָק וּלְיִשְׂרָאֵל עֲבָדֶיךָ

אֲשֶׁר נִשְׁבַּעְתָּ לָהֶם בָּךְ וַתְּדַבֵּר אֲלֵהֶם

אַרְבֶּה אֶת־זַרְעֲכֶם כְּכוֹכְבֵי הַשָּׁמָיִם

וְכָל־הָאָרֶץ הַזֹּאת אֲשֶׁר אָמַרְתִּי אֶתֵּן לְזַרְעֲכֶם

וְנָחֲלוּ לְעֹלָם:

דברים ט זְכֹר לַעֲבָדֶיךָ לְאַבְרָהָם לְיִצְחָק וּלְיַעֲקֹב

אַל־תֵּפֶן אֶל־קְשִׁי הָעָם הַזֶּה וְאֶל־רִשְׁעוֹ וְאֶל־חַטָּאתוֹ:

שליח ציבור: *The*

אֵל נָא תָשֵׁת עָלֵינוּ חַטָּאת

אֲשֶׁר נוֹאַלְנוּ וַאֲשֶׁר חָטָאנוּ:

במדבר יב

קהל: *The*

חָטָאנוּ צוּרֵנוּ, סְלַח לָנוּ יוֹצְרֵנוּ.

All:

זְכֹר Remember the covenant of our fathers, as You have said,
"I will remember My covenant with Jacob,   *Lev. 26*
 and also My covenant with Isaac,
 and also My covenant with Abraham I will remember,
 and the land I will remember."

Remember the covenant of the early ones, as You have said,
"I shall remember for them the covenant of the early ones,   *Lev. 26*
 whom I brought out of the land of Egypt
 before the eyes of the nations,
 in order to be their God: I am the Lord."

Deal kindly with us as You have promised,
"Even so, when they are in the land of their enemies   *Ibid.*
 I shall not reject them
 and shall not detest them to the point of destruction,
 to the point of breaking My covenant with them,
 for I am the Lord their God."

Restore our fortunes and have compassion for us, as it is written:
"And the Lord your God shall restore your fortunes   *Deut. 30*
 and have compassion for you,
 and shall return and gather you in from all the nations
 among whom the Lord your God has scattered you."

Gather those of us who have been distanced, as is written,
"If your distanced ones are at the very ends of the heavens,   *Ibid.*
 from there shall the Lord your God gather you;
 from there shall He bring you."

Wipe out our transgressions as if they were a cloud,
 as if they were a haze, as is written,
"I have wiped out your transgressions like a cloud,   *Is. 44*
 and as a haze your sins;
 come back to Me for I have redeemed you."

All:

ויקרא כו

זְכֹר לָנוּ בְּרִית אָבוֹת כַּאֲשֶׁר אָמַרְתָּ:

וְזָכַרְתִּי אֶת־בְּרִיתִי יַעֲקוֹב

וְאַף אֶת־בְּרִיתִי יִצְחָק וְאַף אֶת־בְּרִיתִי אַבְרָהָם אֶזְכֹּר

וְהָאָרֶץ אֶזְכֹּר:

ויקרא כו

זְכֹר לָנוּ בְּרִית רִאשׁוֹנִים כַּאֲשֶׁר אָמַרְתָּ:

וְזָכַרְתִּי לָהֶם בְּרִית רִאשׁוֹנִים

אֲשֶׁר הוֹצֵאתִי־אוֹתָם מֵאֶרֶץ מִצְרַיִם לְעֵינֵי הַגּוֹיִם

לִהְיוֹת לָהֶם לֵאלֹהִים, אֲנִי יהוה:

ויקרא כו

עֲשֵׂה עִמָּנוּ כְּמוֹ שֶׁהִבְטַחְתָּנוּ:

וְאַף גַּם־זֹאת בִּהְיוֹתָם בְּאֶרֶץ אֹיְבֵיהֶם

לֹא־מְאַסְתִּים וְלֹא־גְעַלְתִּים לְכַלֹּתָם

לְהָפֵר בְּרִיתִי אִתָּם

כִּי אֲנִי יהוה אֱלֹהֵיהֶם:

דברים ל

הָשֵׁב שְׁבוּתֵנוּ וְרַחֲמֵנוּ כְּמוֹ שֶׁכָּתוּב:

וְשָׁב יהוה אֱלֹהֶיךָ אֶת־שְׁבוּתְךָ וְרִחֲמֶךָ

וְשָׁב וְקִבֶּצְךָ מִכָּל־הָעַמִּים

אֲשֶׁר הֱפִיצְךָ יהוה אֱלֹהֶיךָ שָׁמָּה:

דברים ל

קַבֵּץ נִדָּחֵינוּ כְּמוֹ שֶׁכָּתוּב:

אִם־יִהְיֶה נִדַּחֲךָ בִּקְצֵה הַשָּׁמָיִם

מִשָּׁם יְקַבֶּצְךָ יהוה אֱלֹהֶיךָ וּמִשָּׁם יִקָּחֶךָ:

ישעיה מד

מְחֵה פְשָׁעֵינוּ כָּעָב וְכֶעָנָן כְּמוֹ שֶׁכָּתוּב:

מָחִיתִי כָעָב פְּשָׁעֶיךָ וְכֶעָנָן חַטֹּאותֶיךָ, שׁוּבָה אֵלַי כִּי גְאַלְתִּיךָ:

Wipe out our transgressions for Your sake, as You have said:
"I, I am the One who shall wipe out   *Is. 43*
 your transgressions for My sake,
 and I shall not recall your sins."

Whiten our sins as snow and as wool, as is written,
"Come now, let us reason together, says the LORD: *Is. 1*
 If your sins are like scarlet,
 they shall be whitened like snow;
 should they be as red as crimson,
 they shall become like wool."

Throw over us pure waters and purify us, as is written,
"I shall throw pure waters over you   *Ezek. 36*
 and you shall be pure.
 I shall purify you of all your impurities
 and of all your idolatry."

Have compassion for us and do not destroy us, as it is written:
"For the LORD your God is a compassionate God;   *Deut. 4*
 He will not forsake you, He will not destroy you,
 and He will not forget the covenant of your fathers,
 that He pledged to them."

Circumcise our hearts to love Your name, as it is written:
"And the LORD your God will circumcise your heart   *Deut. 30*
 and the heart of your descendants
 to love the LORD your God with all your heart
 and with all your soul, so that you shall live."

Let us find You when we seek You, as it is written:
"And if from there you seek the LORD your God,   *Deut. 4*
 you shall find Him,
 when you seek Him out with all your heart
 and with all your soul."

מְחֵה פְשָׁעֵינוּ לְמַעַנְךָ כַּאֲשֶׁר אָמַרְתָּ:

ישעיה מג
אָנֹכִי אָנֹכִי הוּא מֹחֶה פְשָׁעֶיךָ לְמַעֲנִי
וְחַטֹּאתֶיךָ לֹא אֶזְכֹּר:

הַלְבֵּן חֲטָאֵינוּ כַּשֶּׁלֶג וְכַצֶּמֶר כְּמוֹ שֶׁכָּתוּב:

ישעיה א
לְכוּ־נָא וְנִוָּכְחָה יֹאמַר יהוה
אִם־יִהְיוּ חֲטָאֵיכֶם כַּשָּׁנִים כַּשֶּׁלֶג יַלְבִּינוּ
אִם־יַאְדִּימוּ כַתּוֹלָע כַּצֶּמֶר יִהְיוּ:

זְרֹק עָלֵינוּ מַיִם טְהוֹרִים וְטַהֲרֵנוּ כְּמוֹ שֶׁכָּתוּב:

יחזקאל לו
וְזָרַקְתִּי עֲלֵיכֶם מַיִם טְהוֹרִים וּטְהַרְתֶּם
מִכֹּל טֻמְאוֹתֵיכֶם וּמִכָּל־גִּלּוּלֵיכֶם אֲטַהֵר אֶתְכֶם:

רַחֵם עָלֵינוּ וְאַל תַּשְׁחִיתֵנוּ כְּמוֹ שֶׁכָּתוּב:

דברים ד
כִּי אֵל רַחוּם יהוה אֱלֹהֶיךָ
לֹא יַרְפְּךָ וְלֹא יַשְׁחִיתֶךָ
וְלֹא יִשְׁכַּח אֶת־בְּרִית אֲבֹתֶיךָ אֲשֶׁר נִשְׁבַּע לָהֶם:

וּמוֹל אֶת לְבָבֵנוּ לְאַהֲבָה אֶת שְׁמֶךָ כְּמוֹ שֶׁכָּתוּב:

דברים ל
וּמָל יהוה אֱלֹהֶיךָ אֶת־לְבָבְךָ וְאֶת־לְבַב זַרְעֶךָ
לְאַהֲבָה אֶת־יהוה אֱלֹהֶיךָ בְּכָל־לְבָבְךָ וּבְכָל־נַפְשְׁךָ
לְמַעַן חַיֶּיךָ:

הִמָּצֵא לָנוּ בְּבַקָּשָׁתֵנוּ כְּמוֹ שֶׁכָּתוּב:

דברים ד
וּבִקַּשְׁתֶּם מִשָּׁם אֶת־יהוה אֱלֹהֶיךָ וּמָצָאתָ
כִּי תִדְרְשֶׁנּוּ בְּכָל־לְבָבְךָ וּבְכָל־נַפְשֶׁךָ:

‣ Bring us to Your holy mountain,
and let us rejoice in Your House of prayer, as is written,
"I shall bring them to My holy mountain,   *Is. 56*
and I shall make them rejoice in My House of prayer;
their offerings and their sacrifices will be accepted,
desired on My altar,
for My House will be called a house of prayer for all peoples."

The Ark is opened.

The following is said responsively, verse by verse.

שְׁמַע קוֹלֵנוּ Listen to our voice, LORD our God.
Spare us and have compassion on us,
and in compassion and favour accept our prayer.

Turn us back, O LORD, to You, and we will return.   *Lam. 5*
Renew our days as of old.

Do not cast us away from You,
and do not take Your holy spirit from us.

Do not cast us away in our old age;
when our strength is gone do not desert us.

End of responsive reading.

Do not desert us, LORD; our God, do not be distant from us.

Give us a sign of good things, and those who hate us shall see it
and be ashamed, for You, LORD, will help us and console us.

Hear our speech, LORD, consider our thoughts.

Quietly:

May the words of our mouths and the meditations of our hearts
find favour before You, LORD, our Rock and Redeemer.

For it is You, LORD, that we have longed for;
You shall answer us, O Master our God.

The Ark is closed.

כְּקֶדֶם – "as of old" – is a reference to the Garden of Eden and that we are praying to be restored to the sin-free environment that prevailed when the world
was first created. In most congregations the Ark is opened for this passage.

‹ תְּבִיאֵנוּ אֶל הַר קָדְשֶׁךָ וְשַׂמְּחֵנוּ בְּבֵית תְּפִלָּתֶךָ כְּמוֹ שֶׁכָּתוּב:

וַהֲבִיאוֹתִים אֶל־הַר קָדְשִׁי וְשִׂמַּחְתִּים בְּבֵית תְּפִלָּתִי

עוֹלֹתֵיהֶם וְזִבְחֵיהֶם לְרָצוֹן עַל־מִזְבְּחִי

כִּי בֵיתִי בֵּית־תְּפִלָּה יִקָּרֵא לְכָל־הָעַמִּים:

ישעיה נו

The ארון קודש *is opened.*

The following is said responsively, verse by verse.

שְׁמַע קוֹלֵנוּ, יהוה אֱלֹהֵינוּ, חוּס וְרַחֵם עָלֵינוּ

וְקַבֵּל בְּרַחֲמִים וּבְרָצוֹן אֶת תְּפִלָּתֵנוּ.

הֲשִׁיבֵנוּ יהוה אֵלֶיךָ וְנָשׁוּבָה, חַדֵּשׁ יָמֵינוּ כְּקֶדֶם:

אַל תַּשְׁלִיכֵנוּ מִלְּפָנֶיךָ, וְרוּחַ קָדְשְׁךָ אַל תִּקַּח מִמֶּנּוּ.

אַל תַּשְׁלִיכֵנוּ לְעֵת זִקְנָה, כִּכְלוֹת כֹּחֵנוּ אַל תַּעַזְבֵנוּ.

איכה ה

End of responsive reading.

אַל תַּעַזְבֵנוּ יהוה, אֱלֹהֵינוּ אַל תִּרְחַק מִמֶּנּוּ.

עֲשֵׂה עִמָּנוּ אוֹת לְטוֹבָה, וְיִרְאוּ שׂוֹנְאֵינוּ וְיֵבֹשׁוּ

כִּי אַתָּה יהוה עֲזַרְתָּנוּ וְנִחַמְתָּנוּ.

אֲמָרֵינוּ הַאֲזִינָה יהוה, בִּינָה הֲגִיגֵנוּ.

Quietly:

יִהְיוּ לְרָצוֹן אִמְרֵי פִינוּ וְהֶגְיוֹן לִבֵּנוּ לְפָנֶיךָ, יהוה צוּרֵנוּ וְגוֹאֲלֵנוּ.

כִּי לְךָ יהוה הוֹחָלְנוּ, אַתָּה תַעֲנֶה אֲדֹנָי אֱלֹהֵינוּ.

The ארון קודש *is closed.*

שְׁמַע קוֹלֵנוּ *Listen to our voice.* After the formal *Seliḥot* have been recited, the service draws to its conclusion with a series of verses and petitions prevailing upon God to listen to and accept the prayers that we have recited. The line commencing *Shema Kolenu* is excerpted from the weekday Amida prayer. Together with the lines that follow, it is recited responsively by the *ḥazan* and congregation with great fervour. The second verse asks God to enable us to return to Him and to restore our days as of old. The commentators explain that

VIDUY

אֱלֹהֵינוּ Our God and God of our fathers,
let our prayer come before You, and do not hide Yourself from our plea,
for we are not so arrogant or obstinate
as to say before You, LORD, our God and God of our fathers,
we are righteous and have not sinned, for in truth,
we and our fathers have sinned.

At each expression, strike the chest on the left side:

אָשַׁמְנוּ We have been guilty, we have acted treacherously,
we have robbed, we have spoken slander.
We have acted perversely, we have acted wickedly,
we have acted presumptuously, we have been violent, we have framed lies.
We have given bad advice, we have deceived, we have scorned,
we have rebelled, we have provoked, we have turned away,
we have committed iniquity, we have transgressed,
we have persecuted, we have been obstinate.
We have acted wickedly, we have corrupted,
we have acted abominably, we have strayed, we have led others astray.

▸ We have turned away from Your commandments and good laws, to no avail, *Neh. 9*
for You are just in all that has befallen us,
for You have acted faithfully while we have done wickedly.

אָשַׁמְנוּ We are the guiltiest of peoples; we are the most shameful of generations; gladness has been banished from us; our hearts are sick from our sins;
our desired place has been demolished; our glory has been ravaged; our
divine abode, our Temple, has been destroyed by our iniquities; our castle
has become wasteland; the beauty of our earth has been seized by strangers;
our power by foreigners. But we have yet to return from the error of our
ways; how can we dare insist before You, O LORD, our God and the God of

---

The concept of *viduy* is inseparable from the concept of repentance.
Rambam (Maimonides) begins his Laws of Teshuva (repentance) by stating
that "If one transgresses any of the mitzvot of the Torah, whether deliber-
ately or inadvertently, when one performs *teshuva* and repents for one's sins,
one must confess before the Almighty." It is impossible for us to improve
ourselves if we do not confront and face up to our wrongdoings. According

וידוי

אֱלֹהֵינוּ וֵאלֹהֵי אֲבוֹתֵינוּ
תָּבֹא לְפָנֶיךָ תְּפִלָּתֵנוּ, וְאַל תִּתְעַלַּם מִתְּחִנָּתֵנוּ.
שֶׁאֵין אָנוּ עַזֵּי פָנִים וּקְשֵׁי עֹרֶף לוֹמַר לְפָנֶיךָ
יהוה אֱלֹהֵינוּ וֵאלֹהֵי אֲבוֹתֵינוּ, צַדִּיקִים אֲנַחְנוּ וְלֹא חָטָאנוּ.
אֲבָל אֲנַחְנוּ (וַאֲבוֹתֵינוּ) חָטָאנוּ.

At each expression, strike the chest on the left side:

אָשַׁמְנוּ, בָּגַדְנוּ, גָּזַלְנוּ, דִּבַּרְנוּ דֹפִי.
הֶעֱוִינוּ, וְהִרְשַׁעְנוּ, זַדְנוּ, חָמַסְנוּ, טָפַלְנוּ שָׁקֶר.
יָעַצְנוּ רָע, כִּזַּבְנוּ, לַצְנוּ, מָרַדְנוּ, נִאַצְנוּ
סָרַרְנוּ, עָוִינוּ, פָּשַׁעְנוּ, צָרַרְנוּ, קִשִּׁינוּ עֹרֶף.
רָשַׁעְנוּ, שִׁחַתְנוּ, תִּעַבְנוּ, תָּעִינוּ, תִּעְתָּעְנוּ.

‹ סַרְנוּ מִמִּצְוֹתֶיךָ וּמִמִּשְׁפָּטֶיךָ הַטּוֹבִים, וְלֹא שָׁוָה לָנוּ.
נחמיה ט וְאַתָּה צַדִּיק עַל כָּל־הַבָּא עָלֵינוּ, כִּי־אֱמֶת עָשִׂיתָ וַאֲנַחְנוּ הִרְשָׁעְנוּ:

אָשַׁמְנוּ מִכָּל עָם, בֹּשְׁנוּ מִכָּל דּוֹר, גָּלָה מִמֶּנּוּ מָשׂוֹשׂ, דָּוָה לִבֵּנוּ בַּחֲטָאֵינוּ,
הֻחְבַּל אֲוּוּיֵנוּ, וְנִפְרַע פְּאֵרֵנוּ, זְבוּל בֵּית מִקְדָּשֵׁנוּ חָרַב בַּעֲוֹנֵינוּ, טִירָתֵנוּ
הָיְתָה לְשַׁמָּה, יֳפִי אַדְמָתֵנוּ לְזָרִים, כֹּחֵנוּ לְנָכְרִים. וַעֲדַיִן לֹא שַׁבְנוּ
מִטָּעוּתֵנוּ, וְהֵיךְ נָעִיז פָּנֵינוּ וְנַקְשֶׁה עָרְפֵּנוּ, לוֹמַר לְפָנֶיךָ, יהוה אֱלֹהֵינוּ

וידוי VIDUY – CONFESSION

The *"Ashamnu, Bagadnu"* confession is known as the "short" *viduy* (confession) in contrast to the much longer and more detailed catalogue of sins (*Al ḥet*) which we recite in the Amida on Yom Kippur. This passage presents an alphabetical list of different modes of sinfulness that we might have engaged in. Acknowledging our deep regret for having erred in our ways, we strike our chest as we mention each mode of sin. Rav Joseph B. Soloveitchik observed that with this short *viduy* we are unequivocally admitting our inexcusable guilt.

our ancestors, that we are righteous, and have not sinned – for we (and our ancestors) have sinned!

At each expression, strike the chest on the left side:

אָשַׁמְנוּ We have been guilty, we have acted treacherously,
we have robbed, we have spoken slander.
We have acted perversely, we have acted wickedly,
we have acted presumptuously, we have been violent, we have framed lies.
We have given bad advice, we have deceived, we have scorned,
we have rebelled, we have provoked, we have turned away,
we have committed iniquity, we have transgressed,
we have persecuted, we have been obstinate.
We have acted wickedly, we have corrupted,
we have acted abominably, we have strayed, we have led others astray.

▸ We have turned away from Your commandments and good laws, to no avail, *Neh. 9*
for You are just in all that has befallen us, for You have acted faithfully while
we have done wickedly.

לְעֵינֵינוּ Before our very eyes, they have exploited our toil; pulled and plucked it
away from us; laid their yoke upon us; we have borne it upon our shoulders;
slaves have ruled over us – there is no one to save us from their hands. So   *Lam. 5*
many troubles surround us; we call out to You, O Lᴏʀᴅ our God; we have
grown distant from You through our sins; we have turned away from You; we
have deviated from the path, and become lost. But we have yet to return from
the error of our ways; how can we dare insist before You, O Lᴏʀᴅ, our God
and the God of our ancestors, that we are righteous, and have not sinned – for
we (and our ancestors) have sinned!

At each expression, strike the chest on the left side:

אָשַׁמְנוּ We have been guilty, we have acted treacherously,
we have robbed, we have spoken slander.
We have acted perversely, we have acted wickedly,
we have acted presumptuously, we have been violent, we have framed lies.
We have given bad advice, we have deceived, we have scorned,
we have rebelled, we have provoked, we have turned away,
we have committed iniquity, we have transgressed,
we have persecuted, we have been obstinate.
We have acted wickedly, we have corrupted,
we have acted abominably, we have strayed, we have led others astray.

וֵאלֹהֵי אֲבוֹתֵינוּ, צַדִּיקִים אֲנַחְנוּ וְלֹא חָטָאנוּ, אֲבָל אֲנַחְנוּ (וַאֲבוֹתֵינוּ)
חָטָאנוּ.

At each expression, strike the chest on the left side:

אָשַׁמְנוּ, בָּגַדְנוּ, גָּזַלְנוּ, דִּבַּרְנוּ דֹפִי.
הֶעֱוִינוּ, וְהִרְשַׁעְנוּ, זַדְנוּ, חָמַסְנוּ, טָפַלְנוּ שֶׁקֶר.
יָעַצְנוּ רָע, כִּזַּבְנוּ, לַצְנוּ, מָרַדְנוּ, נִאַצְנוּ
סָרַרְנוּ, עָוִינוּ, פָּשַׁעְנוּ, צָרַרְנוּ, קִשִּׁינוּ עֹרֶף.
רָשַׁעְנוּ, שִׁחַתְנוּ, תִּעַבְנוּ, תָּעִינוּ, תִּעְתָּעְנוּ.

‹ סַרְנוּ מִמִּצְוֹתֶיךָ וּמִמִּשְׁפָּטֶיךָ הַטּוֹבִים, וְלֹא שָׁוָה לָנוּ. וְאַתָּה צַדִּיק עַל   נחמיה ט
כָּל־הַבָּא עָלֵינוּ, כִּי־אֱמֶת עָשִׂיתָ וַאֲנַחְנוּ הִרְשָׁעְנוּ:

לְעֵינֵינוּ עָשְׁקוּ עֲמָלֵנוּ, מְמֻשָּׁךְ וּמְמֹרָט מִמֶּנּוּ, נָתְנוּ עֻלָּם עָלֵינוּ, סָבַלְנוּ
עַל שִׁכְמֵנוּ, עֲבָדִים מָשְׁלוּ בָנוּ, פֹּרֵק אֵין מִיָּדָם: צָרוֹת רַבּוֹת סְבָבוּנוּ,   איכה ה
קְרָאנוּךָ יהוה אֱלֹהֵינוּ, רָחַקְתָּ מִמֶּנּוּ בַּעֲוֹנֵינוּ, שַׁבְנוּ מֵאַחֲרֶיךָ, תָּעִינוּ
וְאָבָדְנוּ. וַעֲדַיִן לֹא שַׁבְנוּ מִטָּעוּתֵנוּ, וְהֵיךְ נָעִיז פָּנֵינוּ וְנַקְשֶׁה עָרְפֵּנוּ,
לוֹמַר לְפָנֶיךָ, יהוה אֱלֹהֵינוּ וֵאלֹהֵי אֲבוֹתֵינוּ, צַדִּיקִים אֲנַחְנוּ וְלֹא חָטָאנוּ,
אֲבָל אֲנַחְנוּ (וַאֲבוֹתֵינוּ) חָטָאנוּ.

At each expression, strike the chest on the left side:

אָשַׁמְנוּ, בָּגַדְנוּ, גָּזַלְנוּ, דִּבַּרְנוּ דֹפִי.
הֶעֱוִינוּ, וְהִרְשַׁעְנוּ, זַדְנוּ, חָמַסְנוּ, טָפַלְנוּ שֶׁקֶר.
יָעַצְנוּ רָע, כִּזַּבְנוּ, לַצְנוּ, מָרַדְנוּ, נִאַצְנוּ
סָרַרְנוּ, עָוִינוּ, פָּשַׁעְנוּ, צָרַרְנוּ, קִשִּׁינוּ עֹרֶף.
רָשַׁעְנוּ, שִׁחַתְנוּ, תִּעַבְנוּ, תָּעִינוּ, תִּעְתָּעְנוּ.

to Rambam, proper *teshuva* means that a person must (i) express regret for
past transgressions, (ii) abandon sinful behaviour, and (iii) commit to being
guiltless in the future.

▸ **סַרְנוּ** We have turned away from Your commandments and good laws, to no *Neh. 9* avail, for You are just in all that has befallen us, for You have acted faithfully while we have done wickedly.

מְשִׁיחַ Your righteous anointed one declared before You: Who can under- *Ps. 19* stand errors? Cleanse me of hidden sins. Cleanse us, O LORD our God, from all our wrongs, and purify us from all our impurities; sprinkle pure water upon us and purify us, as it is stated by Your prophets: "I shall sprinkle pure *Ezek. 36* water upon you and you shall be purified from all your impurities; and from all your fixations I shall purify you. Your people and Your portion hunger for Your goodness, thirst for Your loving-kindness, crave Your salvation. Let them recognise and know that the LORD, our God, has compassion and forgiveness.

> **אֵל רַחוּם** Compassionate God is Your name.
> Gracious God is Your name.
> We are called by Your name.
> LORD, act for the sake of Your name.

Act for the sake of Your truth. Act for the sake of Your covenant. Act for the sake of Your greatness and glory. Act for the sake of Your Law. Act for the sake of Your majesty. Act for the sake of Your promise. Act for the sake of Your remembrance. Act for the sake of Your loving-kindness. Act for the sake of Your goodness. Act for the sake of Your Oneness. Act for the sake of Your honour. Act for the sake of Your wisdom. Act for the sake of Your kingship. Act for the sake of Your eternity. Act for the sake of Your mystery. Act for the sake of Your might. Act for the sake of Your splendour. Act for the sake of Your righteousness. Act for the sake of Your holiness. Act for the sake of Your great compassion. Act for the sake of Your Presence. Act for the sake of Your praise.

Act for the sake of those who loved You, who now dwell in the dust. Act for the sake of Abraham, Isaac and Jacob. Act for the sake of Moses and Aaron. Act for the sake of David and Solomon. Act for the sake of Jerusalem, Your holy city. Act for the sake of Zion, the dwelling place of Your glory. Act for the sake of the desolate site of Your Temple. Act for the sake of the ruins of Your altar. Act for the sake of those killed in sanctification of Your name. Act for the sake of those slaughtered over Your unity. Act for the sake of those who have gone through fire and water in sanctification of Your name.

‹ סָרְנוּ מִמִּצְוֹתֶיךָ וּמִמִּשְׁפָּטֶיךָ הַטּוֹבִים, וְלֹא שָׁוָה לָנוּ. וְאַתָּה צַדִּיק עַל כָּל־הַבָּא עָלֵינוּ, כִּי־אֱמֶת עָשִׂיתָ וַאֲנַחְנוּ הִרְשָׁעְנוּ: נחמיה ט

מְשִׁיחַ צִדְקֶךָ אָמַר לְפָנֶיךָ: שְׁגִיאוֹת מִי־יָבִין, מִנִּסְתָּרוֹת נַקֵּנִי: נַקֵּנוּ יהוה תהלים יט אֱלֹהֵינוּ מִכָּל פְּשָׁעֵינוּ וְטַהֲרֵנוּ מִכָּל טֻמְאוֹתֵינוּ וּזְרֹק עָלֵינוּ מַיִם טְהוֹרִים וְטַהֲרֵנוּ, כַּכָּתוּב עַל יַד נְבִיאֶךָ: וְזָרַקְתִּי עֲלֵיכֶם מַיִם טְהוֹרִים וּטְהַרְתֶּם, יחזקאל לו מִכֹּל טֻמְאוֹתֵיכֶם וּמִכָּל־גִּלּוּלֵיכֶם אֲטַהֵר אֶתְכֶם: עַמְּךָ וְנַחֲלָתְךָ רְעֵבֵי טוּבְךָ, צְמֵאֵי חַסְדְּךָ, תְּאֵבֵי יִשְׁעֶךָ. יַכִּירוּ וְיֵדְעוּ, כִּי לַיהוה אֱלֹהֵינוּ הָרַחֲמִים וְהַסְּלִיחוֹת.

אֵל רַחוּם שְׁמֶךָ.

אֵל חַנּוּן שְׁמֶךָ.

בָּנוּ נִקְרָא שְׁמֶךָ.

יהוה עֲשֵׂה לְמַעַן שְׁמֶךָ.

עֲשֵׂה לְמַעַן אֲמִתָּךְ. עֲשֵׂה לְמַעַן בְּרִיתָךְ. עֲשֵׂה לְמַעַן גָּדְלָךְ וְתִפְאַרְתָּךְ. עֲשֵׂה לְמַעַן דָּתָךְ. עֲשֵׂה לְמַעַן הוֹדָךְ. עֲשֵׂה לְמַעַן וְעוּדָךְ. עֲשֵׂה לְמַעַן זִכְרָךְ. עֲשֵׂה לְמַעַן חַסְדָּךְ. עֲשֵׂה לְמַעַן טוּבָךְ. עֲשֵׂה לְמַעַן יִחוּדָךְ. עֲשֵׂה לְמַעַן כְּבוֹדָךְ. עֲשֵׂה לְמַעַן לִמּוּדָךְ. עֲשֵׂה לְמַעַן מַלְכוּתָךְ. עֲשֵׂה לְמַעַן נִצְחָךְ. עֲשֵׂה לְמַעַן סוֹדָךְ. עֲשֵׂה לְמַעַן עֻזָּךְ. עֲשֵׂה לְמַעַן פְּאֵרָךְ. עֲשֵׂה לְמַעַן צִדְקָתָךְ. עֲשֵׂה לְמַעַן קְדֻשָּׁתָךְ. עֲשֵׂה לְמַעַן רַחֲמֶיךָ הָרַבִּים. עֲשֵׂה לְמַעַן שְׁכִינָתָךְ. עֲשֵׂה לְמַעַן תְּהִלָּתָךְ.

עֲשֵׂה לְמַעַן אוֹהֲבֶיךָ שׁוֹכְנֵי עָפָר. עֲשֵׂה לְמַעַן אַבְרָהָם יִצְחָק וְיַעֲקֹב. עֲשֵׂה לְמַעַן מֹשֶׁה וְאַהֲרֹן. עֲשֵׂה לְמַעַן דָּוִד וּשְׁלֹמֹה. עֲשֵׂה לְמַעַן יְרוּשָׁלַיִם עִיר קָדְשֶׁךָ. עֲשֵׂה לְמַעַן צִיּוֹן מִשְׁכַּן כְּבוֹדֶךָ. עֲשֵׂה לְמַעַן שִׁמְמוֹת הֵיכָלֶךָ. עֲשֵׂה לְמַעַן הֲרִיסוּת מִזְבְּחֶךָ. עֲשֵׂה לְמַעַן הֲרוּגִים עַל שֵׁם קָדְשֶׁךָ. עֲשֵׂה לְמַעַן טְבוּחִים עַל יִחוּדֶךָ. עֲשֵׂה לְמַעַן בָּאֵי בָאֵשׁ וּבַמַּיִם עַל קִדּוּשׁ

Act for the sake of suckling infants who have not sinned. Act for the sake of little ones just weaned who have done no wrong. Act for the sake of schoolchildren. Act for Your own sake if not for ours. Act for Your own sake, and save us.

עֲנֵנוּ Answer us, LORD, answer us. Answer us, our God, answer us.

Answer us, our Father, answer us. Answer us, our Creator, answer us. Answer us, our Redeemer, answer us. Answer us, You who seek us, answer us. Answer us, God who is faithful, answer us. Answer us, You who are ancient and kind, answer us. Answer us, You who are pure and upright, answer us. Answer us, You who are alive and remain, answer us. Answer us, You who are good and do good, answer us. Answer us, You who know our impulses, answer us. Answer us, You who conquer rage, answer us. Answer us, You who clothe Yourself in righteousness, answer us. Answer us, Supreme King of kings, answer us. Answer us, You who are awesome and elevated, answer us. Answer us, You who forgive and pardon, answer us. Answer us, You who answer in times of trouble, answer us. Answer us, You who redeem and save, answer us. Answer us, You who are righteous and straightforward, answer us. Answer us, You who are close to those who call, answer us. Answer us, You who are compassionate and gracious, answer us. Answer us, You who listen to the destitute, answer us. Answer us, You who support the innocent, answer us. Answer us, God of our fathers, answer us. Answer us, God of Abraham, answer us. Answer us, Terror of Isaac, answer us. Answer us, Champion of Jacob, answer us. Answer us, Help of the tribes, answer us. Answer us, Stronghold of the mothers, answer us. Answer us, You who are slow to anger, answer us. Answer us, You who are lightly appeased, answer us. Answer us, You who answer at times of favour, answer us. Answer us, Father of orphans, answer us. Answer us, Justice of widows, answer us.

מִי שֶׁעָנָה The One who answered Abraham our father on Mount Moriah – answer us.
The One who answered Isaac his son, when he was bound upon the altar – answer us.
The One who answered Jacob in Beth-El – answer us.

---

of the golden calf, and Elijah's prayer on Mount Carmel when he was pitted against the prophets of Baal. Others are based on Midrashic traditions or the

שְׁמֶךָ. עֲשֵׂה לְמַעַן יוֹנְקֵי שָׁדַיִם שֶׁלֹּא חָטָאוּ. עֲשֵׂה לְמַעַן גְּמוּלֵי חָלָב
שֶׁלֹּא פָשָׁעוּ. עֲשֵׂה לְמַעַן תִּינוֹקוֹת שֶׁל בֵּית רַבָּן. עֲשֵׂה לְמַעַנְךָ אִם לֹא
לְמַעֲנֵנוּ. עֲשֵׂה לְמַעַנְךָ וְהוֹשִׁיעֵנוּ.

עֲנֵנוּ יהוה עֲנֵנוּ. עֲנֵנוּ אֱלֹהֵינוּ עֲנֵנוּ.

עֲנֵנוּ אָבִינוּ עֲנֵנוּ. עֲנֵנוּ בּוֹרְאֵנוּ עֲנֵנוּ. עֲנֵנוּ גּוֹאֲלֵנוּ עֲנֵנוּ. עֲנֵנוּ דּוֹרְשֵׁנוּ
עֲנֵנוּ. עֲנֵנוּ הָאֵל הַנֶּאֱמָן עֲנֵנוּ. עֲנֵנוּ וָתִיק וְחָסִיד עֲנֵנוּ. עֲנֵנוּ זַךְ וְיָשָׁר
עֲנֵנוּ. עֲנֵנוּ חַי וְקַיָּם עֲנֵנוּ. עֲנֵנוּ טוֹב וּמֵטִיב עֲנֵנוּ. עֲנֵנוּ יוֹדֵעַ יֵצֶר עֲנֵנוּ.
עֲנֵנוּ כּוֹבֵשׁ כְּעָסִים עֲנֵנוּ. עֲנֵנוּ לוֹבֵשׁ צְדָקוֹת עֲנֵנוּ. עֲנֵנוּ מֶלֶךְ מַלְכֵי
הַמְּלָכִים עֲנֵנוּ. עֲנֵנוּ נוֹרָא וְנִשְׂגָּב עֲנֵנוּ. עֲנֵנוּ סוֹלֵחַ וּמוֹחֵל עֲנֵנוּ. עֲנֵנוּ
עוֹנֶה בְּעֵת צָרָה עֲנֵנוּ. עֲנֵנוּ פּוֹדֶה וּמַצִּיל עֲנֵנוּ. עֲנֵנוּ צַדִּיק וְיָשָׁר עֲנֵנוּ.
עֲנֵנוּ קָרוֹב לְקוֹרְאָיו עֲנֵנוּ. עֲנֵנוּ רַחוּם וְחַנּוּן עֲנֵנוּ. עֲנֵנוּ שׁוֹמֵעַ אֶל אֶבְיוֹנִים
עֲנֵנוּ. עֲנֵנוּ תּוֹמֵךְ תְּמִימִים עֲנֵנוּ. עֲנֵנוּ אֱלֹהֵי אֲבוֹתֵינוּ עֲנֵנוּ. עֲנֵנוּ אֱלֹהֵי
אַבְרָהָם עֲנֵנוּ. עֲנֵנוּ פַּחַד יִצְחָק עֲנֵנוּ. עֲנֵנוּ אֲבִיר יַעֲקֹב עֲנֵנוּ. עֲנֵנוּ עֶזְרַת
הַשְּׁבָטִים עֲנֵנוּ. עֲנֵנוּ מִשְׂגָּב אִמָּהוֹת עֲנֵנוּ. עֲנֵנוּ קָשֶׁה לִכְעֹס עֲנֵנוּ. עֲנֵנוּ
רַךְ לִרְצוֹת עֲנֵנוּ. עֲנֵנוּ עוֹנֶה בְּעֵת רָצוֹן עֲנֵנוּ. עֲנֵנוּ אֲבִי יְתוֹמִים עֲנֵנוּ.
עֲנֵנוּ דַּיַּן אַלְמָנוֹת עֲנֵנוּ.

מִי שֶׁעָנָה לְאַבְרָהָם אָבִינוּ בְּהַר הַמּוֹרִיָּה, הוּא יַעֲנֵנוּ.
מִי שֶׁעָנָה לְיִצְחָק בְּנוֹ כְּשֶׁנֶּעֱקַד עַל גַּבֵּי הַמִּזְבֵּחַ, הוּא יַעֲנֵנוּ.
מִי שֶׁעָנָה לְיַעֲקֹב בְּבֵית אֵל, הוּא יַעֲנֵנוּ.

מִי שֶׁעָנָה *The One who answered*. This final *Seliḥa* is based on the Mishna
(*Taʾanit* 2:4) which details the additional *berakhot* that were recited on public
fast days. We note that God has answered the prayers of the Jewish people on
numerous occasions during the course of history and we beseech Him to do
so yet again for us. Some of the examples in this passage are obvious refer-
ences to biblical events, such as Moses' prayer at Mount Sinai after the sin

The One who answered Joseph in prison – answer us.

The One who answered our fathers at the Reed Sea – answer us.

The One who answered Moses at Horeb – answer us.

The One who answered Aaron over his firepan – answer us.

The One who answered Pinehas when he stood up from among
                                        the congregation – answer us.

The One who answered Joshua at Gilgal – answer us.

The One who answered Samuel at Mitzpah – answer us.

The One who answered David and Solomon his son in Jerusalem –
                                        answer us.

The One who answered Elijah on Mount Carmel – answer us.

The One who answered Elisha at Jericho – answer us.

The One who answered Jonah in the belly of the fish – answer us.

The One who answered Hezekiah the king of Judah in his illness –
                                        answer us.

The One who answered Hananiah, Mishael and Azariah in the furnace of
                                        fire – answer us.

The One who answered Daniel in the lions' den – answer us.

The One who answered Mordekhai and Esther in Shushan the capital city
                                        – answer us.

The One who answered Ezra in his exile – answer us.

The One who answered so many righteous, devoted, innocent and upright
                                        people – answer us.

▸ רַחֲמָנָא Merciful One, who answers the oppressed: answer us.

Merciful One, who answers the broken hearted: answer us.

Merciful One, who answers those of humbled spirit: answer us.

Merciful One, answer us.

Merciful One, spare; Loving God, release; Loving God, save us.

Merciful One, have compassion for us now, swiftly,
                    at a time soon coming.

---

assumptions of the author. The passage concludes with an Aramaic petition
echoing the same theme that God – described here as רַחֲמָנָא, the Merciful
One – should answer our prayers and redeem us.

מִי שֶׁעָנָה לְיוֹסֵף בְּבֵית הָאֲסוּרִים, הוּא יַעֲנֵנוּ.
מִי שֶׁעָנָה לַאֲבוֹתֵינוּ עַל יַם סוּף, הוּא יַעֲנֵנוּ.
מִי שֶׁעָנָה לְמֹשֶׁה בְּחוֹרֵב, הוּא יַעֲנֵנוּ.
מִי שֶׁעָנָה לְאַהֲרֹן בַּמַּחְתָּה, הוּא יַעֲנֵנוּ.
מִי שֶׁעָנָה לְפִינְחָס בְּקוּמוֹ מִתּוֹךְ הָעֵדָה, הוּא יַעֲנֵנוּ.
מִי שֶׁעָנָה לִיהוֹשֻׁעַ בַּגִּלְגָּל, הוּא יַעֲנֵנוּ.
מִי שֶׁעָנָה לִשְׁמוּאֵל בַּמִּצְפָּה, הוּא יַעֲנֵנוּ.
מִי שֶׁעָנָה לְדָוִד וּשְׁלֹמֹה בְנוֹ בִּירוּשָׁלַיִם, הוּא יַעֲנֵנוּ.
מִי שֶׁעָנָה לְאֵלִיָּהוּ בְּהַר הַכַּרְמֶל, הוּא יַעֲנֵנוּ.
מִי שֶׁעָנָה לֶאֱלִישָׁע בִּירִיחוֹ, הוּא יַעֲנֵנוּ.
מִי שֶׁעָנָה לְיוֹנָה בִּמְעֵי הַדָּגָה, הוּא יַעֲנֵנוּ.
מִי שֶׁעָנָה לְחִזְקִיָּהוּ מֶלֶךְ יְהוּדָה בְּחָלְיוֹ, הוּא יַעֲנֵנוּ.
מִי שֶׁעָנָה לַחֲנַנְיָה מִישָׁאֵל וַעֲזַרְיָה בְּתוֹךְ כִּבְשַׁן הָאֵשׁ, הוּא יַעֲנֵנוּ.
מִי שֶׁעָנָה לְדָנִיֵּאל בְּגוֹב הָאֲרָיוֹת, הוּא יַעֲנֵנוּ.
מִי שֶׁעָנָה לְמָרְדְּכַי וְאֶסְתֵּר בְּשׁוּשַׁן הַבִּירָה, הוּא יַעֲנֵנוּ.
מִי שֶׁעָנָה לְעֶזְרָא בַּגּוֹלָה, הוּא יַעֲנֵנוּ.
מִי שֶׁעָנָה לְכָל הַצַּדִּיקִים וְהַחֲסִידִים וְהַתְּמִימִים וְהַיְשָׁרִים הוּא יַעֲנֵנוּ.

‹ רַחֲמָנָא דְּעָנֵי לַעֲנִיֵּי עֲנֵינָא.
רַחֲמָנָא דְּעָנֵי לִתְבִירֵי לִבָּא עֲנֵינָא.
רַחֲמָנָא דְּעָנֵי לְמַכִּיכֵי רוּחָא עֲנֵינָא.
רַחֲמָנָא עֲנֵינָא.
רַחֲמָנָא חוּס, רַחֲמָנָא פְּרֹק, רַחֲמָנָא שֵׁיזִב.
רַחֲמָנָא רַחֵם עֲלָן
הַשְׁתָּא בַּעֲגָלָא וּבִזְמַן קָרִיב.

LOWERING THE HEAD

Compassionate and Gracious One, I have sinned before You.
Lord, full of compassion,
have compassion on me and accept my pleas.

Lord, do not rebuke me in Your anger or chastise me in Your wrath.   *Ps. 6*
Be gracious to me, Lord, for I am weak.
Heal me, Lord, for my bones are in agony.
My soul is in anguish, and You, O Lord – how long?
Turn, Lord, set my soul free; save me for the sake of Your love.
For no one remembers You when he is dead.
Who can praise You from the grave?
I am weary with my sighing.
Every night I drench my bed, I soak my couch with my tears.
My eye grows dim from grief, worn out because of all my foes.
Leave me, all you evildoers,
for the Lord has heard the sound of my weeping.
The Lord has heard my pleas. The Lord will accept my prayer.
All my enemies will be shamed and utterly dismayed.
They will turn back in sudden shame.

מְחִי O He who strikes down and who heals, who deals death and brings
to life, who raises up from Sheol (hell) into eternal life. When a son sins,
his father beats him; our Father, who has compassion, heals our pain.
When a slave rebels, he suffers in chains; if his master desires his return,
he breaks his chains. We are Your firstborn, and we have sinned before
You; our souls are brimming with bitter wormwood. We are your slaves,
and we have rebelled before You; some have suffered plunder, some have
suffered captivity, some have suffered lashing. Please, in Your abundant
mercy, heal the pain that torments us, so we will not perish in captivity.

---

prostration was practised in antiquity. Chief Rabbi Hertz commented that
the precise content of this psalm is less important than the symbolism of
the position that we assume, which is "symbolic of complete humiliation
before God, and committing of our destinies entirely into His hands. This
is the moment for the worshipper to give utterance before God to his most
secret hopes and needs."

נפילת אפיים

רַחוּם וְחַנּוּן, חָטָאתִי לְפָנֶיךָ.
יהוה מָלֵא רַחֲמִים, רַחֵם עָלַי וְקַבֵּל תַּחֲנוּנָי.

תהלים ו

יהוה, אַל־בְּאַפְּךָ תוֹכִיחֵנִי, וְאַל־בַּחֲמָתְךָ תְיַסְּרֵנִי:
חָנֵּנִי יהוה, כִּי אֻמְלַל אָנִי, רְפָאֵנִי יהוה, כִּי נִבְהֲלוּ עֲצָמָי:
וְנַפְשִׁי נִבְהֲלָה מְאֹד, וְאַתָּ יהוה, עַד־מָתָי:
שׁוּבָה יהוה, חַלְּצָה נַפְשִׁי, הוֹשִׁיעֵנִי לְמַעַן חַסְדֶּךָ:
כִּי אֵין בַּמָּוֶת זִכְרֶךָ, בִּשְׁאוֹל מִי יוֹדֶה־לָּךְ:
יָגַעְתִּי בְּאַנְחָתִי, אַשְׂחֶה בְכָל־לַיְלָה מִטָּתִי
בְּדִמְעָתִי עַרְשִׂי אַמְסֶה:
עָשְׁשָׁה מִכַּעַס עֵינִי, עָתְקָה בְּכָל־צוֹרְרָי:
סוּרוּ מִמֶּנִּי כָּל־פֹּעֲלֵי אָוֶן, כִּי שָׁמַע יהוה קוֹל בִּכְיִי:
שָׁמַע יהוה תְּחִנָּתִי, יהוה תְּפִלָּתִי יִקָּח:
יֵבֹשׁוּ וְיִבָּהֲלוּ מְאֹד כָּל־אֹיְבָי, יָשֻׁבוּ יֵבֹשׁוּ רָגַע:

מָחֵי וּמַסֵּי, מֵמִית וּמְחַיֶּה, מַסִּיק מִשְּׁאוֹל לְחַיֵּי עָלְמָא. בְּרָא כַּד חֲטֵי,
אֲבוּהִי לַקְיֵהּ, אֲבוּהִי דְּחָיֵּיס מַסֵּי לְכְאֵבֵהּ. עַבְדָּא דְּמָרֵיד נָפִיק בְּקוֹלָר,
מָרֵהּ תָּאִיב וְתָבַר קוֹלָרֵהּ. בְּרָךְ בִּכְרָךְ אֲנַן וְחָטֵינַן קָמָךְ, רַוְיָא נַפְשָׁן
בְּגִדִּין מָרִין. עַבְדָּךְ אֲנַן וּמְרוֹדְנַן קָמָךְ, הָא בְּבִזְיָתָא הָא בִּשְׁבִיתָא
וְהָא בְּמַלְקִיּוּתָא. בְּמָטוּ מִנָּךְ בְּרַחֲמָךְ דְּנְפִישִׁין, אַסֵּי לִכְאֵיבִין דְּתַקּוֹף
עֲלָן, עַד דְּלָא נֶהֱוֵי גְּמִירָא בְּשִׁבְיָא.

נפילת אפיים LOWERING THE HEAD

Psalm 6, with additional introductory verses, is part of our weekday Shaḥarit
and Minḥa services, serving as an additional supplication following the
Amida. If there is a *Sefer Torah* in the room the worshippers rest their heads
on their forearms in a mode of submission, reminiscent of how complete

Agents of mercy, bear our pleas for mercy before the Master of mercy. Proclaimers of prayer, proclaim our prayers before He who hears prayer. Sounders of cries, sound our cries before He who hears cries. Agents of tears, bear our tears before the King who is appeased by tears. Strive and intensify supplication and plea before the exalted, supreme divine King. Mention before Him – sound before Him – the Torah and good deeds of those who dwell in dust. May He recall their love, and let their children live, so the remnant of Jacob will not be lost. For the flock of the faithful shepherd has become a disgrace, a byword among the nations. Answer us swiftly, O LORD our God; redeem us from all harsh decrees; save Your righteous anointed one and Your people, in Your abundant mercy.

Master in heaven, to You we plead, like a captive pleads to his captor: captives are redeemed through ransom, while Your people, the house of Israel, are redeemed through mercy and supplication. Grant our request and our desire; do not send us away empty-handed.

Master in heaven, to You we plead, like a slave pleads to his master: we are exploited, engulfed in darkness. Our souls are bitter from so much hardship. It is not within our power to appease You, O Master. Act for the sake of the promise; for the covenant You formed with our ancestors.

שׁוֹמֵר יִשְׂרָאֵל Guardian of Israel, guard the remnant of Israel,
and let not Israel perish, who declare, "Listen, Israel."

Guardian of a unique nation, guard the remnant of a unique people,
and let not that unique nation perish, who proclaim the unity
of Your name [saying], "The LORD is our God, the LORD is One."

Guardian of a holy nation, guard the remnant of that holy people,
and let not the holy nation perish, who three times repeat
the threefold declaration of holiness to the Holy One.

---

the grounds that it suggests that we are praying to angels, rather than to God. Others endorsed it, saying that it is clear that we are pleading to the angels to entreat the Almighty on our behalf. The Maharal of Prague suggested altering the text slightly, whilst the Ḥatam Sofer validated the traditional text, but wrote that he spent longer reciting the previous paragraphs and personally omitted this passage.

מַכְנִיסֵי רַחֲמִים, הַכְנִיסוּ רַחֲמֵינוּ לִפְנֵי בַּעַל הָרַחֲמִים. מַשְׁמִיעֵי תְפִלָּה,
הַשְׁמִיעוּ תְפִלָּתֵנוּ לִפְנֵי שׁוֹמֵעַ תְּפִלָּה. מַשְׁמִיעֵי צְעָקָה, הַשְׁמִיעוּ צַעֲקָתֵנוּ
לִפְנֵי שׁוֹמֵעַ צְעָקָה. מַכְנִיסֵי דִמְעָה, הַכְנִיסוּ דִמְעוֹתֵינוּ לִפְנֵי מֶלֶךְ מִתְרַצֶּה
בִדְמָעוֹת. הִשְׁתַּדְּלוּ וְהַרְבּוּ תְחִנָּה וּבַקָּשָׁה לִפְנֵי מֶלֶךְ אֵל רָם וְנִשָּׂא.
הַזְכִּירוּ לְפָנָיו הַשְׁמִיעוּ לְפָנָיו תּוֹרָה וּמַעֲשִׂים טוֹבִים שֶׁל שׁוֹכְנֵי עָפָר.
יִזְכֹּר אַהֲבָתָם וִיחַיֶּה זַרְעָם, שֶׁלֹּא תֹאבַד שְׁאֵרִית יַעֲקֹב. כִּי צֹאן רוֹעֶה
נֶאֱמָן הָיָה לְחֶרְפָּה, יִשְׂרָאֵל גּוֹי אֶחָד לְמָשָׁל וְלִשְׁנִינָה. מַהֵר עֲנֵנוּ יהוה
אֱלֹהֵינוּ, וּפְדֵנוּ מִכָּל גְּזֵרוֹת קָשׁוֹת, וְהוֹשִׁיעָה בְּרַחֲמֶיךָ הָרַבִּים מְשִׁיחַ
צִדְקְךָ וְעַמֶּךָ.

מָרָן דְּבִשְׁמַיָּא לָךְ מִתְחַנְּנַן, כְּבַר שַׁבְיָא דְּמִתְחַנֵּן לְמָרֵהּ: כֻּלְּהוֹן בְּנֵי
שַׁבְיָא בְּכַסְפָּא מִתְפָּרְקִין, וְעַמָּךְ בֵּית יִשְׂרָאֵל בְּרַחֲמֵי וּבְתַחֲנוּנֵי. הַב
לַן שְׁאֶלְתָּן וּבָעוּתָן, דְּלָא נֶהֱדַר רֵיקָם מִן קָדָמָךְ.

מָרָן דְּבִשְׁמַיָּא לָךְ מִתְחַנְּנַן, כְּעַבְדָּא דְּמִתְחַנֵּן לְמָרֵהּ: עֲשִׁיקֵי אֲנָן
וּבַחֲשׁוֹכָא שָׁרֵינַן. מְרִירָן נַפְשָׁן מֵעַקְתִין דִּנְפִישִׁין. חֵילָא לֵית בָּן לְרַצּוּיָךְ,
מָרָן. עֲבִיד בְּדִיל קְיָמָא דִּגְזַרְתְּ עִם אֲבָהָתָנָא.

שׁוֹמֵר יִשְׂרָאֵל, שְׁמֹר שְׁאֵרִית יִשְׂרָאֵל, וְאַל יֹאבַד יִשְׂרָאֵל
הָאוֹמְרִים שְׁמַע יִשְׂרָאֵל.
שׁוֹמֵר גּוֹי אֶחָד, שְׁמֹר שְׁאֵרִית עַם אֶחָד, וְאַל יֹאבַד גּוֹי אֶחָד
הַמְיַחֲדִים שִׁמְךָ, יהוה אֱלֹהֵינוּ יהוה אֶחָד.
שׁוֹמֵר גּוֹי קָדוֹשׁ, שְׁמֹר שְׁאֵרִית עַם קָדוֹשׁ, וְאַל יֹאבַד גּוֹי קָדוֹשׁ
הַמְשַׁלְּשִׁים בְּשָׁלֹשׁ קְדֻשּׁוֹת לְקָדוֹשׁ.

מַכְנִיסֵי רַחֲמִים *Agents of mercy.* As the *Seliḥot* service nears conclusion we ask the ministering angels to assist us by presenting our prayers and supplications before the Almighty. This prayer, clearly of ancient composition, appears in the ninth-century siddur of Rav Amram Gaon. Its inclusion in the *Seliḥot* service has caused centuries of controversy. Some authorities opposed it on

You who are conciliated by calls for compassion and placated by pleas,
    be conciliated and placated towards an afflicted generation,
    for there is no other help.

Our Father, our King, be gracious to us and answer us, though we have
    no worthy deeds; act with us in charity and loving-kindness and
    save us.

Stand at ^.

וַאֲנַחְנוּ We do not know ^what to do, but our eyes are turned to You. *11 Chr. 12*
Remember, LORD, Your compassion and loving-kindness, for they *Ps. 25*
are everlasting. May Your loving-kindness, LORD, be with us, for we *Ps. 33*
have put our hope in You. Do not hold against us the sins of those who *Ps. 79*
came before us. May Your mercies meet us swiftly, for we have been
brought very low. Be gracious to us, LORD, be gracious to us, for we are *Ps. 123*
sated with contempt. In wrath, remember mercy. He knows our nature; *Hab. 3* / *Ps. 103*
He remembers that we are dust. ▸ Help us, God of our salvation, for the *Ps. 79*
sake of the glory of Your name. Save us and grant atonement for our sins
for Your name's sake.

FULL KADDISH

Leader: יִתְגַּדַּל Magnified and sanctified may His great name be,
    in the world He created by His will.
    May He establish His kingdom
    in your lifetime and in your days,
    and in the lifetime of all the house of Israel,
    swiftly and soon –
    and say: Amen.

All: May His great name be blessed for ever and all time.

Leader: Blessed and praised, glorified and exalted,
    raised and honoured,
    uplifted and lauded be
    the name of the Holy One,
    blessed be He,

מִתְרַצֶּה בְּרַחֲמִים וּמִתְפַּיֵּס בְּתַחֲנוּנִים, הִתְרַצֵּה וְהִתְפַּיֵּס לְדוֹר עָנִי כִּי אֵין עוֹזֵר.

אָבִינוּ מַלְכֵּנוּ, חָנֵּנוּ וַעֲנֵנוּ, כִּי אֵין בָּנוּ מַעֲשִׂים עֲשֵׂה עִמָּנוּ צְדָקָה וָחֶסֶד וְהוֹשִׁיעֵנוּ.

Stand at ⌃.

דברי הימים ב' כ"ו
תהלים כה

וַאֲנַחְנוּ לֹא נֵדַע 'מַה־נַּעֲשֶׂה, כִּי עָלֶיךָ עֵינֵינוּ: זְכֹר־רַחֲמֶיךָ יהוה

תהלים לג

וַחֲסָדֶיךָ, כִּי מֵעוֹלָם הֵמָּה: יְהִי־חַסְדְּךָ יהוה עָלֵינוּ, כַּאֲשֶׁר יִחַלְנוּ לָךְ:

תהלים עט
תהלים קכב
חבקוק ג
תהלים קג
תהלים עט

אַל־תִּזְכָּר־לָנוּ עֲוֹנֹת רִאשֹׁנִים מַהֵר יְקַדְּמוּנוּ רַחֲמֶיךָ, כִּי דַלּוֹנוּ מְאֹד: חָנֵּנוּ יהוה חָנֵּנוּ, כִּי־רַב שָׂבַעְנוּ בוּז: בְּרֹגֶז רַחֵם תִּזְכּוֹר: כִּי־הוּא יָדַע יִצְרֵנוּ, זָכוּר כִּי־עָפָר אֲנָחְנוּ: ⌃ עָזְרֵנוּ אֱלֹהֵי יִשְׁעֵנוּ עַל־דְּבַר כְּבוֹד־שְׁמֶךָ, וְהַצִּילֵנוּ וְכַפֵּר עַל־חַטֹּאתֵינוּ לְמַעַן שְׁמֶךָ:

קדיש שלם

ש"ץ: יִתְגַּדַּל וְיִתְקַדַּשׁ שְׁמֵהּ רַבָּא (קהל: אָמֵן)

בְּעָלְמָא דִּי בְרָא כִרְעוּתֵהּ

וְיַמְלִיךְ מַלְכוּתֵהּ

בְּחַיֵּיכוֹן וּבְיוֹמֵיכוֹן וּבְחַיֵּי דִּי כָל בֵּית יִשְׂרָאֵל

בַּעֲגָלָא וּבִזְמַן קָרִיב

וְאִמְרוּ אָמֵן. (קהל: אָמֵן)

קהל
 וש"ץ: יְהֵא שְׁמֵהּ רַבָּא מְבָרַךְ לְעָלַם וּלְעָלְמֵי עָלְמַיָּא.

ש"ץ: יִתְבָּרַךְ וְיִשְׁתַּבַּח וְיִתְפָּאַר וְיִתְרוֹמַם וְיִתְנַשֵּׂא וְיִתְהַדָּר וְיִתְעַלֶּה וְיִתְהַלָּל

שְׁמֵהּ דִּי קֻדְשָׁא בְּרִיךְ הוּא (קהל: בְּרִיךְ הוּא)

beyond any blessing,
song, praise and consolation
uttered in the world –
and say: Amen.

May the prayers and pleas of all Israel
be accepted by their Father in heaven –
and say: Amen.

May there be great peace from heaven,
and life for us and all Israel –
and say: Amen.

*Bow, take three steps back, as if taking leave of the Divine Presence,
then bow, first left, then right, then centre, while saying:*
May He who makes peace in His high places,
make peace for us and all Israel –
and say: Amen.

When Seliḥot are said at midnight "Aleinu" is added.

Stand while saying Aleinu. Bow at ˇ.
עָלֵינוּ It is our duty to praise the Master of all,
and ascribe greatness to the Author of creation,
who has not made us like the nations of the lands,
nor placed us like the families of the earth;
who has not made our portion like theirs,
nor our destiny like all their multitudes.
ˇBut we bow in worship
and thank the Supreme King of kings,
the Holy One, blessed be He,
who extends the heavens
and establishes the earth,
whose throne of glory is in the heavens above,
and whose power's Presence is in the highest of heights.

לְעֵלָּא מִן כָּל בִּרְכָתָא וְשִׁירָתָא, תֻּשְׁבְּחָתָא וְנֶחָמָתָא
דִּי אֲמִירָן בְּעָלְמָא
וְאִמְרוּ אָמֵן. (קהל: אָמֵן)

תִּתְקַבֵּל צְלוֹתְהוֹן וּבָעוּתְהוֹן דִּי כָל בֵּית יִשְׂרָאֵל
קֳדָם אֲבוּהוֹן דִּי בִשְׁמַיָּא
וְאִמְרוּ אָמֵן. (קהל: אָמֵן)

יְהֵא שְׁלָמָא רַבָּא מִן שְׁמַיָּא
וְחַיִּים (טוֹבִים) עָלֵינוּ וְעַל כָּל יִשְׂרָאֵל
וְאִמְרוּ אָמֵן. (קהל: אָמֵן)

*Bow, take three steps back, as if taking leave of the Divine Presence,
then bow, first left, then right, then centre, while saying:*

עֹשֶׂה שָׁלוֹם בִּמְרוֹמָיו
הוּא יַעֲשֶׂה שָׁלוֹם, עָלֵינוּ וְעַל כָּל יִשְׂרָאֵל
וְאִמְרוּ אָמֵן. (קהל: אָמֵן)

When סליחות are said at midnight עָלֵינוּ is added.

Stand while saying עָלֵינוּ. Bow at ˙.

עָלֵינוּ לְשַׁבֵּחַ לַאֲדוֹן הַכֹּל, לָתֵת גְּדֻלָּה לְיוֹצֵר בְּרֵאשִׁית
שֶׁלֹּא עָשָׂנוּ כְּגוֹיֵי הָאֲרָצוֹת, וְלֹא שָׂמָנוּ כְּמִשְׁפְּחוֹת הָאֲדָמָה
שֶׁלֹּא שָׂם חֶלְקֵנוּ כָּהֶם וְגוֹרָלֵנוּ כְּכָל הֲמוֹנָם.
˙וַאֲנַחְנוּ כּוֹרְעִים וּמִשְׁתַּחֲוִים וּמוֹדִים
לִפְנֵי מֶלֶךְ מַלְכֵי הַמְּלָכִים, הַקָּדוֹשׁ בָּרוּךְ הוּא
שֶׁהוּא נוֹטֶה שָׁמַיִם וְיוֹסֵד אָרֶץ
וּמוֹשַׁב יְקָרוֹ בַּשָּׁמַיִם מִמַּעַל
וּשְׁכִינַת עֻזּוֹ בְּגָבְהֵי מְרוֹמִים.

He is our God; there is no other.
Truly He is our King; there is none else,
as it is written in His Torah:
"You shall know and take to heart this day that the LORD is God,   *Deut. 4*
in the heavens above and on the earth below.
There is no other."

Therefore, we place our hope in You, LORD our God,
that we may soon see the glory of Your power,
when You will remove abominations from the earth,
and idols will be utterly destroyed,
when the world will be perfected
under the sovereignty of the Almighty,
when all humanity will call on Your name,
to turn all the earth's wicked towards You.
All the world's inhabitants will realise and know
that to You every knee must bow and every tongue swear loyalty.
Before You, LORD our God, they will kneel and bow down
and give honour to Your glorious name.
They will all accept the yoke of Your kingdom,
and You will reign over them soon and for ever.
For the kingdom is Yours,
and to all eternity You will reign in glory,
as it is written in Your Torah:
"The LORD will reign for ever and ever."   *Ex. 15*
‣ And it is said: "Then the LORD shall be King over all the earth;   *Zech. 14*
on that day the LORD shall be One and His name One."

Some add:

Have no fear of sudden terror or of the ruin when it overtakes the wicked.   *Prov. 3*
Devise your strategy, but it will be thwarted;   *Is. 8*
propose your plan, but it will not stand, for God is with us.
When you grow old, I will still be the same.   *Is. 46*
When your hair turns grey, I will still carry you.
I made you, I will bear you, I will carry you, and I will rescue you.

הוּא אֱלֹהֵינוּ, אֵין עוֹד.

אֱמֶת מַלְכֵּנוּ, אֶפֶס זוּלָתוֹ

כַּכָּתוּב בְּתוֹרָתוֹ, וְיָדַעְתָּ הַיּוֹם וַהֲשֵׁבֹתָ אֶל־לְבָבֶךָ

כִּי יהוה הוּא הָאֱלֹהִים בַּשָּׁמַיִם מִמַּעַל וְעַל־הָאָרֶץ מִתָּחַת

אֵין עוֹד:

עַל כֵּן נְקַוֶּה לְּךָ יהוה אֱלֹהֵינוּ, לִרְאוֹת מְהֵרָה בְּתִפְאֶרֶת עֻזֶּךָ

לְהַעֲבִיר גִּלּוּלִים מִן הָאָרֶץ, וְהָאֱלִילִים כָּרוֹת יִכָּרֵתוּן

לְתַקֵּן עוֹלָם בְּמַלְכוּת שַׁדַּי.

וְכָל בְּנֵי בָשָׂר יִקְרְאוּ בִשְׁמֶךָ לְהַפְנוֹת אֵלֶיךָ כָּל רִשְׁעֵי אָרֶץ.

יַכִּירוּ וְיֵדְעוּ כָּל יוֹשְׁבֵי תֵבֵל

כִּי לְךָ תִּכְרַע כָּל בֶּרֶךְ, תִּשָּׁבַע כָּל לָשׁוֹן.

לְפָנֶיךָ יהוה אֱלֹהֵינוּ יִכְרְעוּ וְיִפֹּלוּ

וְלִכְבוֹד שִׁמְךָ יְקָר יִתֵּנוּ

וִיקַבְּלוּ כֻלָּם אֶת עֹל מַלְכוּתֶךָ

וְתִמְלֹךְ עֲלֵיהֶם מְהֵרָה לְעוֹלָם וָעֶד.

כִּי הַמַּלְכוּת שֶׁלְּךָ הִיא וּלְעוֹלְמֵי עַד תִּמְלֹךְ בְּכָבוֹד

כַּכָּתוּב בְּתוֹרָתֶךָ, יהוה יִמְלֹךְ לְעֹלָם וָעֶד:

◄ וְנֶאֱמַר, וְהָיָה יהוה לְמֶלֶךְ עַל־כָּל־הָאָרֶץ

בַּיּוֹם הַהוּא יִהְיֶה יהוה אֶחָד וּשְׁמוֹ אֶחָד:

Some add:

אַל־תִּירָא מִפַּחַד פִּתְאֹם וּמִשֹּׁאַת רְשָׁעִים כִּי תָבֹא:

עֻצוּ עֵצָה וְתֻפָר, דַּבְּרוּ דָבָר וְלֹא יָקוּם, כִּי עִמָּנוּ אֵל:

וְעַד־זִקְנָה אֲנִי הוּא, וְעַד־שֵׂיבָה אֲנִי אֶסְבֹּל

אֲנִי עָשִׂיתִי וַאֲנִי אֶשָּׂא וַאֲנִי אֶסְבֹּל וַאֲמַלֵּט:

MOURNER'S KADDISH

The following prayer requires the presence of a minyan.

Mourner: יִתְגַּדַּל Magnified and sanctified
may His great name be,
in the world He created by His will.
May He establish His kingdom
in your lifetime and in your days,
and in the lifetime of all the house of Israel,
swiftly and soon –
and say: Amen.

All: May His great name be blessed
for ever and all time.

Mourner: Blessed and praised,
glorified and exalted,
raised and honoured,
uplifted and lauded
be the name of the Holy One,
blessed be He,
beyond any blessing, song,
praise and consolation
uttered in the world –
and say: Amen.

May there be great peace from heaven,
and life for us and all Israel –
and say: Amen.

*Bow, take three steps back, as if taking leave of the Divine Presence,
then bow, first left, then right, then centre, while saying:*
May He who makes peace in His high places,
make peace for us and all Israel –
and say: Amen.

קדיש יתום

The following prayer requires the presence of a מנין.

אבל: יִתְגַּדַּל וְיִתְקַדַּשׁ שְׁמֵהּ רַבָּא (קהל: אָמֵן)

בְּעָלְמָא דִּי בְרָא כִרְעוּתֵהּ

וְיַמְלִיךְ מַלְכוּתֵהּ

בְּחַיֵּיכוֹן וּבְיוֹמֵיכוֹן וּבְחַיֵּי דִּי כָל בֵּית יִשְׂרָאֵל

בַּעֲגָלָא וּבִזְמַן קָרִיב

וְאִמְרוּ אָמֵן. (קהל: אָמֵן)

קהל
ואבל: יְהֵא שְׁמֵהּ רַבָּא מְבָרַךְ לְעָלַם וּלְעָלְמֵי עָלְמַיָּא.

אבל: יִתְבָּרַךְ וְיִשְׁתַּבַּח וְיִתְפָּאַר וְיִתְרוֹמַם וְיִתְנַשֵּׂא

וְיִתְהַדָּר וְיִתְעַלֶּה וְיִתְהַלָּל

שְׁמֵהּ דְּקֻדְשָׁא בְּרִיךְ הוּא (קהל: בְּרִיךְ הוּא)

לְעֵלָּא מִן כָּל בִּרְכָתָא וְשִׁירָתָא, תֻּשְׁבְּחָתָא וְנֶחֱמָתָא

דִּי אֲמִירָן בְּעָלְמָא

וְאִמְרוּ אָמֵן. (קהל: אָמֵן)

יְהֵא שְׁלָמָא רַבָּא מִן שְׁמַיָּא

וְחַיִּים, עָלֵינוּ וְעַל כָּל יִשְׂרָאֵל

וְאִמְרוּ אָמֵן. (קהל: אָמֵן)

*Bow, take three steps back, as if taking leave of the Divine Presence,
then bow, first left, then right, then centre, while saying:*

עֹשֶׂה שָׁלוֹם בִּמְרוֹמָיו

הוּא יַעֲשֶׂה שָׁלוֹם עָלֵינוּ וְעַל כָּל יִשְׂרָאֵל

וְאִמְרוּ אָמֵן. (קהל: אָמֵן)

קוֹרֶן יְרוּשָׁלַיִם